**W9-BWF-329**

## DATE DUE

| | | | |
|---|---|---|---|
| | | | |
| | | | |
| | | | |
| | | | |
| | | | |
| | | | |
| | | | |
| | | | |
| | | | |
| | | | |
| | | | |
| | | | |

921
HAN        Kramer, Barbara
           Tom Hanks : superstar

*Morrill School Library*
*Chicago Public Schools*
*6011 S. Rockwell*
*Chicago, IL 60629*

# Tom Hanks

# The People to Know Series

**Madeleine Albright**
First Woman
Secretary of State
0-7660-1143-7

**Neil Armstrong**
The First Man
on the Moon
0-89490-828-6

**Isaac Asimov**
Master of
Science Fiction
0-7660-1031-7

**Robert Ballard**
Oceanographer Who
Discovered the Titanic
0-7660-1147-X

**Barbara Bush**
First Lady
0-89490-350-0

**Willa Cather**
Writer of the Prairie
0-89490-980-0

**Bill Clinton**
United States President
0-89490-437-X

**Hillary Rodham Clinton**
Activist First Lady
0-89490-583-X

**Bill Cosby**
Actor and Comedian
0-89490-548-1

**Walt Disney**
Creator of Mickey Mouse
0-89490-694-1

**Bob Dole**
Legendary Senator
0-89490-825-1

**Marian Wright Edelman**
Fighting for
Children's Rights
0-89490-623-2

**Bill Gates**
Billionaire
Computer Genius
0-89490-824-3

**Ruth Bader Ginsberg**
Supreme Court Justice
0-89490-621-6

**John Glenn**
Astronaut and Senator
Revised Edition
0-7660-1532-7

**Jane Goodall**
Protector of
Chimpanzees
0-89490-827-8

**Al Gore**
Leader for the
New Millennium
0-7660-1232-8

**Tipper Gore**
Activist, Author,
Photographer
0-7660-1142-9

**Billy Graham**
World-Famous Evangelist
0-7660-1533-5

**Alex Haley**
Author of Roots
0-89490-573-2

**Ernest Hemingway**
Writer and Adventurer
0-89490-979-7

**Ron Howard**
Child Star &
Hollywood Director
0-89490-981-9

**Helen Keller**
Lighting the Way for
the Blind and Deaf
0-7660-1530-0

**John F. Kennedy**
President of the
New Frontier
0-89490-693-3

**Stephen King**
King of Thrillers
and Horror
0-7660-1233-6

**John Lennon**
The Beatles and Beyond
0-89490-702-6

**Maya Lin**
Architect and Artist
0-89490-499-X

**Jack London**
A Writer's
Adventurous Life
0-7660-1144-5

**Malcolm X**
A Voice for Black America
0-89490-435-3

**Wilma Mankiller**
Leader of the
Cherokee Nation
0-89490-498-1

**Branford Marsalis**
Jazz Musician
0-89490-495-7

**Anne McCaffrey**
Science Fiction Storyteller
0-7660-1151-8

**Barbara McClintock**
Nobel Prize Geneticist
0-89490-983-5

**Rosie O'Donnell**
Talk Show Host
and Comedian
0-7660-1148-8

**Gary Paulsen**
Author and Wilderness
Adventurer
0-7660-1146-1

**Christopher Reeve**
Hollywood's Man
of Courage
0-7660-1149-6

**Ann Richards**
Politician, Feminist,
Survivor
0-89490-497-3

**Sally Ride**
First American Woman
in Space
0-89490-829-4

**Will Rogers**
Cowboy Philosopher
0-89490-695-X

**Franklin D. Roosevelt**
The Four-Term President
0-89490-696-8

**Steven Spielberg**
Hollywood Filmmaker
0-89490-697-6

**John Steinbeck**
America's Author
0-7660-1150-X

**Martha Stewart**
Successful Businesswoman
0-89490-984-3

**Amy Tan**
Author of
The Joy Luck Club
0-89490-699-2

**Alice Walker**
Author of
The Color Purple
0-89490-620-8

**Andy Warhol**
Pioneer of Pop Art
0-7660-1531-9

**Simon Wiesenthal**
Tracking Down
Nazi Criminals
0-89490-830-8

**Elie Wiesel**
Voice from the Holocaust
0-89490-428-0

**Frank Lloyd Wright**
Visionary Architect
0-7660-1032-X

People to Know

# Tom Hanks

## Superstar

Barbara Kramer

**Enslow Publishers, Inc.**

40 Industrial Road          PO Box 38
Box 398                Aldershot
Berkeley Heights, NJ 07922    Hants GU12 6BP
USA                        UK

http://www.enslow.com

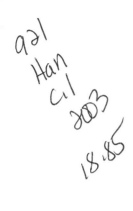

**Library of Congress Cataloging-in-Publication Data**

Kramer, Barbara.
   Tom Hanks : superstar / by Barbara Kramer.
      p. cm. — (People to know)
   Includes bibliographical references and index.
   Summary: Discusses the life of Tom Hanks including his various talents as film
actor, director, writer, and producer.
   ISBN 0-7660-1436-3
   1. Hanks, Tom—Juvenile literature. 2. Actors—United States—Biography—
Juvenile literature. [1. Hanks, Tom. 2. Actors and actresses.] I. Title. II. Series.
PN2287.H18 K73   2001
791.43'028'092—dc21                                    00-008795

Printed in the United States of America

10 9 8 7 6 5 4 3 2 1

**To Our Readers:**
All Internet addresses in this book were active and appropriate when we went to press.
Any comments or suggestions can be sent by e-mail to Comments@enslow.com or to
the address on the back cover.

# Contents

*Tom Hanks*

# "Stupid Is as Stupid Does"

It is a memorable movie scene: An awkward-looking man sits woodenly on a bus stop bench. He is dressed in a white suit and dirty tennis shoes, with his blue-and-white-checked shirt buttoned tight at the neck. The man sits very straight and his hair is shaved high on each side, far above his ears. When a woman sits down at the other end of the bench, he introduces himself. "My name is Forrest, Forrest Gump," he says in his slow, southern drawl.[1] Then Forrest Gump, played by actor Tom Hanks, begins to tell his story to a succession of strangers as they sit alongside him on the bench waiting for their buses.

Gump peppers his amazing story with bits of wisdom from his mother. She taught him how to survive in this world. Gump has a low IQ—limited intelligence—but he does not allow anyone to call him stupid. "Stupid is as stupid does," he says.[2] Even smart people do stupid things.

"Life is like a box of chocolates. You never know what you're going to get," Gump says, and his life has certainly been an assortment.[3] In spite of his low IQ, he has some impressive achievements. He was a star runner on his college football team. He was awarded a Medal of Honor for his heroic actions during the Vietnam War, and he became a table tennis champion, representing the United States in China. In making the movie, the special effects team used computer-generated imaging (CGI) to place Gump in actual news film taken during recent U.S. history. He is shown shaking hands with three presidents—John F. Kennedy, Lyndon Johnson, and Richard Nixon.

Gump becomes a successful businessman as the owner of Bubba Gump Shrimp. Then one day, "for no particular reason," he decides to go out for a run.[4] He runs to one coast and then turns around and heads back to the opposite coast. Gump runs for more than three years, but no one seems to think this is odd. In fact, he picks up followers along the way, who begin running with him.

If you stop to think about it, the story of Forrest Gump makes no sense at all. However, most movie-goers did not think about it; they just enjoyed it. *Forrest Gump* was the "feel good" movie of the summer of 1994. Gump, a simple, decent human being who always keeps his promises, became a new American hero, and Tom Hanks became one of the best-loved actors in the country.

*Forrest Gump* was the highest-grossing non-science-fiction film in history. That record was not broken until 1998, when the movie *Titanic* hit the theaters. Hanks won an Oscar for his performance as Gump. He had already won an Oscar the previous year for his portrayal of Andrew Beckett, a lawyer dying of AIDS in the movie *Philadelphia*. Hanks was the first actor in more than fifty years to win back-to-back Oscars for Best Actor. The only other actor with that distinction was Spencer Tracy, who won for his roles in *Captains Courageous* (1937) and *Boys Town* (1938).

For Hanks, life truly became a box of chocolates. In fact, it became thousands of boxes of chocolate as people began sending him candy. Pleading that he could not eat even one more chocolate, he gave the candy away to friends, coworkers, and anyone who would take some. Hanks was a star, but regular people found him approachable. They shouted at him when they saw him on the street. "Run, Forrest, run!" they called, quoting a line from the movie.[5]

In his stage and film roles, Hanks has led a life almost as fantastic as Gump's. He began his career as a stage actor performing in Shakespearean plays. For two seasons, he played a man who spent much of his time dressed as a woman in the TV situation comedy *Bosom Buddies*. In films, he has starred as a man who falls in love with a mermaid and as a twelve-year-old boy trapped in a man's body. He has been a washed-up baseball player who becomes the manager of a women's

*"Life is like a box of chocolates," says Forrest Gump, played by Tom Hanks. "You never know what you're going to get."*

baseball team and a lonely widower who finds romance at the top of the Empire State Building. He has traveled into space and leaped into a flaming volcano.

Many stars say that as children they dreamed of becoming actors. Hanks was not one of them. Although he later said that his childhood had prepared him for the life of an actor, he did not think about a career in acting until he was in college.

# The New Kid
# in School

$T$om Hanks was born in Concord, California, on July 9, 1956. He was Amos and Janet Hanks's third child. His mother worked as a waitress and his dad worked as a restaurant cook. They divorced when Tom was five years old. Hanks does not remember a lot about the divorce. He just recalls his father loading him and his older brother and sister and some of their stuff into a truck. "I do remember wanting to take all the toys in my closet, but we could only take one or two," Hanks said.[1] They drove off in the middle of the night, headed for Reno, Nevada. There, his dad had a job as a chef in a casino. It was one of many moves over the next few years as Amos Hanks went from job to job.

Tom's younger brother, Jimmy, who was six

months old at that time, stayed with Janet Hanks. Years later, Tom Hanks asked his parents why they chose to split up the family that way. "The answer I got was, you do what you have to do at the time," he said. "I think it was mostly because of money and that neither of them could handle four kids at one time."[2]

Amos Hanks married a woman who had five children. It was a huge change for Tom to suddenly be part of a large family. "I remember in school we had to draw a picture of our house and family and I ran out of places to put people. I put them on the roof," he said.[3]

It also meant that he had to compete with his siblings for attention. "There were these extremely large dinners," Hanks recalled. "You could get lost in the shuffle or you could be a loudmouth. I chose the latter route."[4]

That marriage lasted only two years. Then Amos Hanks and his three children moved back to California. They eventually settled in Oakland, across the bay from San Francisco.

In 1966, Tom's life changed again when Amos Hanks married Frances Wong, who had three daughters. Tom had a hard time adjusting to his father's third marriage. He and his older brother and sister had been living alone with their dad for two and a half years. Amos Hanks worked nights, so the three children were on their own and very independent. They cooked dinner and did the laundry. They were also supposed to keep the house clean, but Hanks says they did not do a very good job.

After enjoying this independence, Tom did not like

having someone telling him what to do. His brother and sister also struggled. Tom's sister, Sandra, who was fifteen years old, decided to go live with their mother. Tom and his older brother Larry stayed with their father, but they moved into the basement of their home, seeing the rest of the family usually only at mealtimes.

Tom's mother, Janet, remarried three times. He saw her on holidays, making the five-hour bus trip to visit her in Red Bluff, California, where she did administrative work for a hospital. "By the time I was ten years old, I had a mother and two stepmothers, I'd lived in ten different houses in five different cities, sometimes with siblings, sometimes without," Hanks recalled.[5]

It was not a typical upbringing, but Hanks does not like reports that say he had an unhappy childhood. "We were just a completely more or less normal broken family," he explained. "Everybody was married a bunch and everybody lived different places, and nobody thought much of it."[6]

The family did not have the problems that Hanks associates with unhappy homes. "My stepfather from 1962 could walk into this room and I wouldn't know him," Hanks explained. "But there was no alcohol and no abuse in my childhood."[7]

In school, Hanks was known as the class clown. "I could make kids laugh standing in line for handball," he recalled.[8] It was an act that he perfected as a way to make up for the shyness of always being the new kid in school. His clowning did not get him into trouble because he knew when to quit. "If the teacher wasn't laughing, I'd shut up," he said.[9]

Although he clowned around at school, at home his brother Larry was known as the funny one. Larry, four years older than Tom, was the one who came up with many of the jokes. But Larry was not as outgoing as Tom was. Tom took his brother's jokes to school and tried them out. When his brother complained, Tom said, "Well, you got to say it out loud, Larry, or it doesn't mean anything."[10]

Tom attended Bret Harte Junior High School in Oakland. By that time, his dad was teaching food and hotel management at a vocational college in the area. He no longer moved from job to job, and Tom was able to attend the same junior high school all three years. However, looking back at his elementary school years, Hanks says that in some ways, he enjoyed the frequent moves. "Just about the time you started getting bored with your apartment, Dad would get another job, and suddenly we would be up and living somewhere else."[11]

He also said that all those moves prepared him for an actor's life. "It made me flexible," he noted. "It gave me confidence to think I can be in any sort of social situation and know how to gracefully get out of it."[12] It also gave him the unique ability to roam freely among the various high school cliques. He managed to fit in with any group of people.

On the other hand, the moves and the changes in Tom's home life did carry a price. Tom was a lonely child, a loneliness that lasted well into his adult life. As a teenager, he joined a church youth group because he felt a need to belong. "I was 14 and needed something very badly—not just something to believe in, not just some sort of faith. I needed a brand of acceptance that would combat the loneliness I had felt all the way up to then."[13]

During the 1960s, Tom got caught up in the excitement of the space race. The United States wanted to be the first country to land a man on the moon before the end of the decade. Tom kept track of all the space flights and could recite each flight's mission and the astronauts on board. He studied constellations and saw the movie *2001: A Space Odyssey* twenty-two times. In 1966, the television series *Star Trek* premiered and Tom became a fan of the show.

Tom attended Skyline High School in Oakland, California, where he was an average student and participated in a couple of sports. "I played soccer for a while and was bad at it, then I ran track and was pretty good at it," he said.[14] Because he was skinny and had long legs, his teammates nicknamed him "Lanky Hanks." He also worked for a short time as a soda vendor at the Oakland A's baseball games.

Tom had a girlfriend, but he recalls that he was not a big hit with girls. "I was death with women in high school—absolutely the strike-out king," he explained. "I was a little too geeky, a little too gangly, and much too manic."[15]

Tom became interested in drama when he saw one of his friends play Dracula in a school play. The next year, Tom signed up for Rawley Farnsworth's drama class. The school did two productions a year—a play in the fall and a musical in the spring. Tom's first role was as a bus driver named Jake Latta in the play *Night of the Iguana*. It was a small part, but even then he made an impression. "He had a great deal of stage presence," Farnsworth noted. "It's the ability to attract an audience when you walk on stage. There are some people that come on stage that you are not that interested in. And there are other people that when they come on, you can't take your eyes off and you want to see everything they do."[16]

Tom's name on the program was spelled Thom Hanks. "I was just trying to be cool," Hanks later said. "As soon as I got out of high school, I said, 'You know what? That's ridiculous,' and changed it back."[17]

In his senior year, Tom made a strong impression playing a character named Luther Billis in the school's production of the musical *South Pacific*. In one scene, he wore a grass skirt, and his shirt was unbuttoned to show a ship painted on his stomach. As he sang and danced, he moved his stomach muscles so that it looked as if the ship were bobbing up and down on the water.

The drama department had a tradition of giving out its own version of the Oscars each year. In March 1974, Tom won the school's "Oscar" for Best Actor. However, he still had no plans to act professionally. "I did some high school shows because they gave me the chance to get on stage and ham it up," he said.[18]

After high school, Hanks enrolled at Chabot Community College, a two-year school in Hayward, California. He also worked part-time as a bellman in a Hilton hotel. At that time he still had no idea what he wanted to do with his life. He says he was "majoring

*As a high school senior, Tom sang and danced in the musical*
South Pacific. *In this scene, his stomach muscles made the*
*painted ship bob up and down.*

in getting up and going to school and waiting for something to conk me on the head and say, 'This is the direction you want to go in.'"[19]

Hanks usually worked a drama class into his schedule each semester because it was fun. One class turned out to be a study of the theater. Students were required to read plays and then attend performances in the San Francisco area. He usually went by himself because his friends were going to basketball games or skiing. In fact, Hanks said he preferred going alone. "I'd just drive to a theater, buy myself a ticket, sit in the seat and read the program, and then get into the play completely," he said.[20]

That class convinced him that he wanted to be part of the theater in some way. In 1976, he transferred to California State University at Sacramento, where he majored in theater arts. At that point, he was not thinking about becoming an actor. "For a time I just wanted to be a stage manager or lighting designer or something like that. I liked stage carpentry, building things; I liked being around the theater."[21] It was there that he met and fell in love with Samantha Lewes, an aspiring actress and producer.

Although Hanks was mainly interested in working behind the scenes, he also acted in plays put on by the university's drama department. One time, when his friends were cast in a play and he was not, he auditioned for a part in *The Cherry Orchard* at the Sacramento Community Theater.

Hanks was chosen to play a servant named Yasha. He also helped build sets for the play. The guest director was Vincent Dowling, who was artistic director of

Great Lakes Shakespeare Festival (later called Great Lakes Theater Festival) in Cleveland, Ohio.

When the play ended, Dowling invited Hanks and some other students to become interns at Great Lakes Shakespeare Festival for the 1977 summer season. Hanks and Lewes traveled to Ohio together. It was an exciting move for Hanks. "It's not like I went out and popped champagne—who could afford champagne?" he said. "But man, I was in a car, and I was driving across the country and I had a job and I was going to be doing something that I love."[22]

# An Ordinary Guy

$A$s a theater intern, Hanks earned no money for his work behind the scenes. However, he soon won acting roles, for which he was paid. When he had time off, Hanks went to baseball games, becoming a Cleveland Indians fan. They were not playing well at the time and did not attract a lot of fans. Hanks did not mind. "I spent a lot of days at the ballpark, in that huge stadium with maybe three thousand people. It was sort of an intimate experience," he said.[1]

That fall, he and Samantha Lewes returned to Sacramento, where Hanks worked as an assistant stage manager at the Sacramento Civic Theater. By that time he had decided on a career in the theater and dropped out of college.

*Building props and sets, Hanks (left) and Bert Goldstein work backstage at Great Lakes Shakespeare Festival in 1977. As a summer intern, Hanks demonstrated his excellent carpentry skills.*

The moving Hanks did as a child carried over into his adult life. For the next few years, he moved often, as he worked to establish himself in the theater. He returned to Ohio for the 1978 summer season. That year, he received the Cleveland Drama Critics Award for his work in the Shakespeare play *The Two Gentlemen of Verona.*

When Great Lakes Shakespeare Festival's summer season ended, Hanks sold his old Volkswagen Beetle for $850. He and Samantha Lewes used the money to move to New York City, where Hanks hoped to make it on Broadway. Lewes was pregnant at the time, and a short while after arriving in New York, she gave birth to their son, Colin. The couple married that year.

At twenty-two, Hanks was an out-of-work actor with a family to support. It was a frightening experience. "I had acting skills but no knowledge of the business," Hanks said. "Didn't even know you had to have a picture and resume."[2]

Hanks was fortunate that his work in Cleveland made him eligible for unemployment. He did not have to work as a waiter or take other jobs that young actors rely on until they get their first big break. He could focus completely on acting, but it was not an easy time. "It was a war of survival, really," Hanks recalled. "I was a kid who had never been in such a big city before. I was on unemployment and trying to act. My wife was an actress as well, and she was pursuing that as best she could."[3]

In 1979, he went back to Ohio for the summer season. In the fall, he returned to New York, where he got a small acting role in the low-budget thriller *He Knows You're Alone*. The movie is about a killer who preys on women who are about to be married. Hanks plays a psychology student.

The movie was shot on Staten Island in New York. Hanks worked only three days to complete his role, which amounted to about seven minutes of on-screen time. "I played this geek who appears out of nowhere in the middle of the movie and then disappears again seven minutes later," he said.[4]

It was not a great film debut. Hanks said the

*Hanks soon won acting roles at Great Lakes Shakespeare Festival. In 1979, he performed with Robert Elliott and Mary Kay Dean in* Do Me a Favorite.

movie was so bad that audiences cheered for the killer. Still, that role led to other work for Hanks. "Somebody from ABC saw it and they asked me to come out to Los Angeles and take part in some new talent program they had," Hanks explained.[5]

Through its talent search, the network offered contracts to promising young actors. Once the actors were signed on, the network tried to work them into new television series. Hanks was flown to Los Angeles, where he stayed in a small hotel and went through a series of screen tests and readings. He returned to New York thinking that he did not have a chance of getting a contract, but he was wrong. Hanks soon received an offer for a lead role in a television pilot. A pilot is a trial show for a new television series. One show of the series is made and shown. Then program executives decide whether to drop the show or to pick it up for the next season.

Hanks auditioned for several series while he was in Los Angeles. He was offered a role in *Bosom Buddies*, which was not even one of the shows he had auditioned for. "I had no idea what I was getting into; if somebody had told me, I would have probably choked," he said.[6]

Hanks flew back to Los Angeles to film the pilot show. When the network selected the series for its fall lineup, Hanks moved his family to the West Coast. Under his agreement with ABC, the network could use him in any of their shows. As a result, he made a guest appearance on the series *The Love Boat* in June 1980. Hanks said that his family all got together to watch that episode. "The good thing about it was I was actually able to be at home, too, and think, 'There I am.'"[7]

*Bosom Buddies* premiered on Thanksgiving night, November 27, 1980. The series was loosely based on the 1959 movie *Some Like It Hot*, starring Tony Curtis, Jack Lemmon, and Marilyn Monroe. Hanks starred as Kip Wilson. Actor Peter Scolari played his friend and coworker, Henry Desmond. In the first episode, these two advertising executives need a place to live after their rat-infested apartment building is demolished. A coworker suggests that they try the hotel where she lives. The price is right. The problem is that it is an all-female hotel. Hanks and Scolari dress up as women, becoming Buffy and Hildegarde to live in the building. Donna Dixon stars as Sonny Lumet, a neighbor who becomes Kip's girlfriend.

Hanks had spent most of his money making the move from New York to Los Angeles. When he started work on *Bosom Buddies*, he was broke. He asked Tom Miller, one of the executive producers of the show, for a $5,000 loan. Miller gave him $10,000. "As soon as Tom received his first paycheck there was only one priority he had: paying the money back," Miller recalled.[8]

Hanks described himself on *Bosom Buddies* as a "lousy actor during the first season."[9] However, the show gave him a chance to work on his comedic skills, and he took advantage of it. Singer-actress Telma Hopkins, who played one of the building's tenants, said the show helped Hanks loosen up. "When I first met Tom, right before we started doing

*When he starred in the television sitcom* Bosom Buddies, *Hanks spent much of his time dressed as a woman.*

the series, he was so serious, I had no idea he could do comedy," she said.[10]

The show had problems. The most obvious was that it was almost impossible to believe that Hanks and Scolari could fool anyone into thinking they were women, even in costume. "Hanks in his Buffy get-up is more like a female moose in distress, and even more preposterous," wrote Robert MacKenzie in a review for *TV Guide*.[11]

On the plus side, the show did have good writing, and Hanks and Scolari worked very well together. From the beginning, they had a good time on the set trying to top each other with ad-libs. Many of their spontaneous lines were worked into the show. "They were very active in suggesting ideas because they're very creative guys," said Leonard Ripps, a writer for the show.[12] Richard Corliss, a critic for *Time* magazine, also commented on the natural talents of the two newcomers. "The young stars, Tom Hanks and Peter Scolari, know when to underplay a line and when to run with it," he wrote.[13]

The series was renewed for a second season, but there were changes in the format. Early in that season, Kip told Sonny that he and Buffy were one and the same person, and the parts where the two men dressed as women were reduced. The change was a relief to Hanks, who says that he hated dressing in drag.

The show developed an almost cultlike following, but there were not enough fans to keep it on the air. *Bosom Buddies* lasted only two seasons, and Hanks was glad when it was over. "I was burned out after two years. Who knows what it would have been like after five?" he said.[14]

Once again, Hanks was looking for work. His family was growing, and he had even more responsibility. Hanks and Lewes had celebrated the birth of their daughter, Elizabeth, in 1981.

Hanks landed the lead role in a television movie, *Mazes and Monsters*, which was broadcast on CBS in December 1982. The movie was based on a Rona Jaffe novel. The idea for Jaffe's book came from a real-life incident in which a college student vanished while playing a fantasy game called Dungeons and Dragons. His rescuers were led through a series of underground tunnels winding beneath the college campus.

In the movie, Hanks plays Robbie Wheeling, a transfer student who flunked out of his previous school because he spent too much time playing the game Mazes and Monsters. It soon becomes evident that he takes the game much too seriously. His personality is taken over by his fantasy character.

A critic for *The New York Times* was unimpressed with the movie, calling it "predictable." However, he was more generous in praising the acting ability of its stars. "The younger actors are required to carry the film and, directed by Steven H. Stern, they do so with remarkable skill," he wrote.[15]

Hanks also made guest appearances on other television series, including a recurring role on the show *Family Ties*, which starred Michael J. Fox. Hanks was Ned O'Donnell, the alcoholic brother of Fox's mother on the show, who was played by Meredith Baxter Birney.

He also guest starred on *Happy Days*, a series starring Ron Howard as 1950s teenager Richie Cunningham. By the time Hanks appeared on the show, Howard had left the series to pursue a career as a director. However, they did get to work together later, when Hanks was cast in *Splash*, a movie Howard was directing.

In *Splash*, Hanks plays Allen Bauer, a wholesaler of fruits and vegetables who falls in love with a mermaid, played by Darryl Hannah. Comedian John Candy is Freddie, Allen Bauer's playboy brother.

Hanks was not Howard's first choice for the romantic lead. "John Candy we always wanted," Howard said. "For his brother we tried to get John Travolta, tried to get Bill Murray, tried to get Dudley Moore, tried to get Chevy Chase. They were all unavailable or not interested. The word was real good on Tom Hanks around town. He read, and he was terrific. We just stopped looking."[16]

Hanks later joked that he got the part only because nobody else wanted it. No matter why he got the part, it was a huge opportunity for Hanks. It was his first major role in a motion picture, and he made the most of it. Howard later remembered Hanks as an actor who was willing to do whatever was asked of him.

On Hanks's first day on the set, Howard took him aside and explained his role. "Tom, your job is not to go toe-to-toe with John Candy and get laughs. If you do that, this movie will stink. Your job is just to love the girl. Just look at her and love her. If we don't believe this girl is magic to you, we don't have a movie."[17]

A movie about a romance between a man and a mermaid required some underwater shooting. The first task for Hanks was learning to feel comfortable under water. Before filming began, he spent about a week learning to scuba dive. That was great fun, but once filming began, reality set in. The scuba gear was taken away, and Hanks and Darryl Hannah had to film their underwater scenes with no oxygen tanks.

Howard set up an underwater lifeline. As soon as the actors finished filming a scene, they swam over to the lifeline to get deep breaths of air. Because they could not talk under water, the actors developed a series of hand signals. Later, Hanks jokingly described those signals to a reporter. He said that when he patted his chest, it meant that he needed air. A thumbs-up signal meant that he wanted up and out of the water. Then, while the reporter looked on, Hanks began flapping his arms wildly, demonstrating the most important signal of all. "That means, 'Help me, I'm dying,'" Hanks explained.[18]

*Splash* became the surprise hit of 1984. It launched the film-acting careers of Darryl Hannah and Tom Hanks, and the directing career of Ron Howard. It appeared that Hanks had done a good job of following Howard's advice. Movie critic Roger Ebert wrote that Hanks is "the kind of guy you can somehow imagine in love with a mermaid."[19] It was also the beginning of the kind of role that Hanks would become noted for—an ordinary guy reacting to the craziness that is going on around him.

In real life, it appeared that Hanks really was that ordinary guy. He said that off camera he enjoyed a quiet life. He liked hanging out at home talking on the telephone, watching television, and reading. "I like boredom—I save the exciting stuff for work," he said.[20]

But Tom Hanks did not have much time to be bored.

# A Filming Frenzy

Hanks's next film, *Bachelor Party*, was also released in 1984. Hanks plays Rick Gassko, a school bus driver who is about to marry. His beautiful and rich bride-to-be is Debbie Thompson, played by Tawny Kitaen. This kind of movie was popular at that time. *Bachelor Party* showed all the silliness that can happen when a group of young men get together to celebrate the bridegroom's last fling before marriage. The movie did not get good reviews, but it did well at the box office.

It was the beginning of a hectic filming schedule for Hanks, who made three movies in rapid succession. *The Man with One Red Shoe* opened in theaters in July 1985. Hanks stars as Richard Drew, a classical violinist who is mistaken for a secret agent.

Although he did not actually play the violin in the movie, Hanks was determined to look convincing. Until then, his only experience with the violin was some lessons in the fifth grade, and he had quit after about six weeks. Before filming began, Hanks spent five months studying the violin, practicing five hours a day. Still, his hard work and a good supporting cast, which included Carrie Fisher and Jim Belushi, could not save a bad movie. It bombed at the box office and with critics. In *People* magazine, Ralph Novak described the movie in one word—"borrrrrring."[1]

Immediately after finishing *The Man with One Red Shoe*, Hanks went to Mexico to film *Volunteers*, released in August 1985. He was reunited with John Candy for that movie. Hanks plays Lawrence Bourne III, a Yale graduate with a gambling problem. To escape his creditors, whom he owes $28,000, Bourne takes his roommate's place as a volunteer in the Peace Corps.

The Peace Corps is an actual organization sponsored by the U.S. government. Volunteers travel to developing countries to help the people with agricultural, educational, and public health projects. But it is doubtful that they have ever had a volunteer quite as spoiled as Lawrence Bourne III.

The film also stars Rita Wilson as Bourne's love interest. Wilson and Hanks had first met during her guest appearance on *Bosom Buddies*. "She played a great computer date who turned out to be a devil worshipper—Cindy 666, I think she was called," Hanks said.[2] In *Volunteers*, she plays Beth Wexler, a fellow volunteer.

*Actors John Candy, Rita Wilson, and Tom Hanks prepare to blow up a bridge in a scene from* Volunteers.

Nicholas Meyer, director of *Volunteers*, later talked about working with Hanks: "He was always very professional; there was nothing you could fault; he would do anything you'd ask him, but he wasn't prepared to reveal himself as a human being."[3]

Others who work with Hanks agree. Hanks is friendly, but most people do not get to know him well. Hanks has said that his desire to keep to himself is probably the result of moving around so much as a child. It did not give him a chance to establish lasting friendships. "I don't think it's part of my mental makeup to completely open myself up to people I know," he explained.[4]

From *Volunteers*, Hanks went straight into

rehearsal for *The Money Pit.* He stars as Walter Fielding, a lawyer for rock and roll groups. Fielding buys and begins renovating a rundown mansion that falls apart faster than repairs can be made. Hanks's costar, Shelley Long, is best known for her role as Diane Chambers on the television series *Cheers.*

The movie relies heavily on special effects, and it was a very physical role for Hanks. In the course of the movie, he falls through a hole in the floor, climbs a staircase that is falling apart beneath him, and has kitchen appliances blow up in his face. In one scene, Hanks is covered in plaster from head to foot. Although critics praised Hanks for his comedic talents, the movie got poor reviews and was disappointing at the box office.

None of Hanks's movies in that period even came close to being as successful as *Splash.* But Hanks had established a good career based on the charm and humor that he had relied on as the new kid in school. "Eventually it became quite a money-making machine for me," he said.[5]

Hanks recognized that he did not yet have the skills to move beyond that type of comedic role, but he was learning. His next movie, *Nothing in Common,* gave him a chance to combine comedy with drama, something he was not ready to do earlier in his career. "It wasn't until *Nothing in Common* that I knew enough to tone it down, rein it in, and start trying to tell the truth, as opposed to just telling a joke," he explained.[6]

*Nothing in Common* was directed by Garry Marshall, who directed *Happy Days* when Hanks made his guest appearance. In *Nothing in Common,*

Hanks plays David Basner, an advertising executive. In typical Tom Hanks fashion, the character uses wisecracks to cover his feelings. That changes when his parents, played by Jackie Gleason and Eva Marie Saint, split up after thirty-six years of marriage. Troubles mount when Basner's father is fired from his job and then hospitalized for complications from diabetes. Basner's parents need him, and in the process of helping them, he also gets in touch with his own feelings.

Hanks had plenty of real-life experience to draw on for his role in *Nothing in Common*. His father had been seriously ill several times with kidney disease. Amos Hanks suffered kidney failure and had to go on dialysis, a treatment to remove waste and excess fluid from the blood when the kidneys fail to do the job. Eventually, he had two kidney transplants. Tom remembered feeling helpless because there was so little he could do for his father, who lay unconscious in a hospital bed. "The only thing I could do was wash his face with a washrag. That does something to you," Hanks said.[7]

He also knew something about the pain of divorce. Although he had not talked about it, there had been problems between Hanks and his wife for some time. He had moved out of their home, but few people on the movie set were aware of his personal troubles because Hanks did not let them affect his work. "He's one of the few young actors who doesn't believe that the set should revolve around his private life," Garry Marshall noted.[8]

By the time *Nothing in Common* was released in

July 1986, Hanks and Rita Wilson, his costar in *Volunteers*, had begun dating. They said that they were attracted to each other when they worked on *Volunteers*. However, at the time, they were both involved in other relationships. Hanks was still trying to work things out with his wife, and Wilson was engaged to be married. They decided to be just friends. Since then their lives had changed. Rita Wilson had broken off her engagement and Hanks's marriage had ended.

Hanks was concerned about how divorce would affect his children. "The first thing that went through my mind was, 'Oh, my God; my kids are going to feel as lonely as I did,'" he said, recalling his own childhood.[9] The divorce also left him with doubts about his ability to have a successful marriage. Those doubts led him to seek professional counseling, attending therapy sessions three times a week for several months.

*Nothing in Common* received little attention, but for Hanks it was an important project. During filming of *The Money Pit*, Hanks had signed a three-movie development deal with Columbia Pictures. According to the agreement, Hanks could find films he wanted to do and bring them to the studio. In return, Hanks would be paid about $1 million for starring in the films. *Nothing in Common* was the first film Hanks made under that agreement. It meant that he was able to work on the film in its planning stages. Because of that, he had input into the kind of character he wanted to play. "It [the movie] really changed me and started

*Hanks attended the 1986 premiere of* Nothing in Common *with actress Rita Wilson.*

me looking at my position in moviemaking in a different way," he said.[10]

Hanks took another serious role in *Every Time We Say Goodbye*, playing a World War II Royal Air Force pilot who is wounded. He spends time recovering in Jerusalem, where he falls in love with a Jewish woman. Filming was done in Israel, and Hanks was the only American in the movie. The movie, released in November 1986, went almost unnoticed in the United States, playing in only a limited number of theaters.

After two serious roles, Hanks was ready for a change. He said that acting in serious films takes "emotional investment, which is very, very exhausting."[11] He took a comedy break with *Dragnet*, which opened in 1987.

*Dragnet* spoofed a former television series with the same name. Dan Aykroyd stars as Sergeant Joe Friday, and Hanks plays Friday's partner, Pep Streebek. Hanks admired Aykroyd's work and said that one reason he made that movie was the chance to work with Aykroyd. The movie was considered a hit at the box office, but Hanks was disappointed with the project, noting that it "could have been funnier."[12]

Although critics were not enthusiastic about some of Hanks's films, most of their reviews of Hanks himself were good. It was something that even Hanks could not explain. "I really don't understand it myself," he said. "I've been very lucky with the press."[13]

He was also a favorite with moviegoers. People were talking about Tom Hanks's appeal, although no one could pinpoint exactly what that was. One reporter described it by writing, "Hanks is an actor who is on best-friends terms with his audience."[14]

Another reporter related it to the type of roles that Hanks played. "His characters seem to thrive on what makes the rest of us crazy; they adjust, cheerfully, to the weirdness of their lives, while taking due note of just how weird it is."[15] But it appeared that what most people liked about Tom Hanks was that he seemed like a regular guy who just happened to be a good actor.

Hanks's star power was growing, bringing its own set of problems. One of those problems was filming on location. "I used to really love working outdoors," he said. "Now it can be uncomfortable. People yell. I like it better when people come over, when you're done, and say 'We like your work.' That's real nice."[16]

His growing popularity also made it difficult for him to go to baseball games. He could no longer just sit back and enjoy the game unnoticed by fans. "It's getting harder now. But I still go out to the ballpark," he said.[17]

In his spare time, Hanks enjoyed playing tennis and he decided to take up golf. "It proved to be really goofy fun, the nuttiest thing in town," Hanks said about golf.[18] "Goofy" is a word that Hanks uses often, as in "I've got a goofy-looking nose,"[19] and "I did seem to get offered an awful lot of goofy, silly roles."[20]

Although some of them were goofy roles, Hanks was very much in demand, getting about twenty scripts a day for his consideration. His agent and his personal manager read them first, picking out the best. Hanks himself looked at about three scripts a day. "You know in the first three pages if you're going to *want* to do the thing or not," he said.[21]

Hanks capped off a busy year by proposing to Rita Wilson on New Year's Eve 1987. The couple was at a restaurant having dinner with friends when Hanks popped the question. "You bet," Wilson answered.[22]

# The *Big* Year

Hanks decided to take a few months off at the beginning of 1988. "There are other things that are just more important than being a hotshot-celebrity movie actor," he explained. "I simply want to pay attention to those other things for a while, things like life and love and going to the bank and organizing your garage."[1] Love was at the top of that list, apparently. He married Rita Wilson on April 30, 1988.

They honeymooned in the Caribbean, but Hanks could not fully enjoy the warm weather. "I had to stay out of the sun because I may be starting a job before the end of May, in which case I can't look too bronzed, so I wore a hat and a lot of sunblock," he said.[2]

Although Hanks was taking a break, it was hardly

noticeable to his fans. He had already completed work on two movies that were released in 1988. The first, *Big,* premiered in June with Hanks in the lead role. He plays Josh Baskin, a twelve-year-old boy who puts a quarter into a wish machine at a carnival. His wish is to be big to impress a girl who is taller than he is. His wish comes true in a way that he never imagined—he wakes up the next morning in Hanks's thirty-something body.

Josh's parents are understandably frightened and confused when a grown man turns up in their son's room, insisting that he is Josh. They accuse him of being their son's kidnapper, which forces Josh to leave home. He travels to New York City, where, because of his computer skills, he lands a job in the data processing department of a toy company. He quickly rises to the top of the company because of his knack for knowing what kids like. Of course, no one else knows that the key to his success is that he actually *likes* playing with the toys.

As with *Splash,* Hanks was not the first choice for that role. The screenplay was written by Anne Spielberg (Steven Spielberg's sister) and Gary Ross. In the planning stages, Steven Spielberg was set to direct the movie with Harrison Ford in the starring role. Those plans fell through when Spielberg and Ford got busy making an Indiana Jones movie. The part was also offered to Robert De Niro, who turned it down.

Hanks got the part after Penny Marshall (sister of director Garry Marshall) was signed to direct the movie. She wanted Hanks. He took the part, even though his agent advised him against it. Trapping a boy in a man's body was a popular film device at the time. With three other similar movies—*Vice Versa*; *Like Father, Like Son*; and *18 Again*—Hanks's agent worried that *Big* would not get much attention. Hanks was willing to take a chance. He noted that there were lots of cop movies where a cop gets killed and his partner solves the crime. "We just had to learn to think of the other films as other 'cop' movies," he said, "and that we were going to make our version."[3]

Penny Marshall was best known as Laverne on the television series *Laverne and Shirley*. She had directed only one other movie, *Jumpin' Jack Flash*, starring Whoopi Goldberg. In spite of her limited experience, Hanks enjoyed working with Marshall. "It's the first time I worked with someone I knew as a friend before I was an employee. It was an enormous help," he said.[4]

On the other hand, Hanks noted that Marshall demanded more rehearsing than any other director he had worked with until then. But the extra work paid off. One of the most memorable scenes in the movie takes place in the famous F.A.O. Schwarz toy store in New York City. There, Hanks and Robert Loggia, who plays his boss at the toy company, dance "Chopsticks" and "Heart and Soul" on a giant keyboard. The segment was carefully choreographed and extensively rehearsed. "It was exhausting, like jumping rope for ten hours," Hanks recalled.[5]

Josh appears to be an adult with a great job and a woman who loves him, but inside he is still a twelve-year-old boy. (He celebrates his thirteenth birthday

*In one of the most memorable scenes in Big, Hanks and Robert Loggia tap out some tunes on a giant keyboard. Filming the scene was "exhausting, like jumping rope for ten hours," said Hanks.*

during the film.) That boy misses his family and friends, which is where *Big* differed from the other movies. The makers of *Big* were not just going for laughs at the weird things that can happen when a child is suddenly thrust into an adult world. There was a tenderness in *Big* that the other movies lacked. "*Big* is big comedy news—that rare film that can tickle the funny bone and touch the heart," wrote Peter Travers in *People* magazine.[6]

Hanks had a good time filming *Big*. "I had to show up on time and that was the last adult thing I had to do for the day," he joked. "The rest of the time, I could goof around and get away with it."[7]

However, in a more serious moment, he admitted that the role was not easy: "It was hard, a hard movie to make. Grueling and long with lots of things to pay attention to."[8]

Hanks drew on several different experiences to prepare himself. He observed David Moscow, the twelve-year-old boy who plays Josh Baskin as a child. He also got ideas from his own children, who were then ten and six years old. "I tried to get a sense from them of play for the sake of play, of having cars on the carpet and having this great time where you make up your own story, your own little world," he said.[9]

Most of all, Hanks said that he remembered what it was like to be a kid. "I think I've always had a pretty good sense of that aspect of my personality anyway. I'm not too overburdened with sophistication that I can't have a good time," he explained.[10]

A bit of the young Josh Baskin came out again when Hanks and Rita Wilson attended a screening of the movie. They sat in the back row of the theater. Hanks wore a Chicago White Sox baseball cap pulled down low to keep from being recognized. The screening was not without problems. Three different times a big blob appeared on the screen when the film got stuck in the projector and the projector bulb melted the film. "Hey!" Hanks called out. "Great effect!"[11]

Otherwise, he was serious during the screening. A reporter later commented that Hanks did not even laugh with the audience at the funny parts. As Wilson and Hanks were leaving the theater, it was obvious that the film had touched them both. "What a sweet movie. I didn't expect to cry," Hanks said.[12]

On the other hand, when a reporter asked Wilson if she ever imagined that Hanks would do such a good job of acting like a twelve-year-old boy, she laughed. "This is a man who plays hockey inside the house with a bag of Milano cookies!" she said, indicating that her husband was plenty capable of acting like a child.[13]

Hanks's second movie in 1988 was filmed before *Big*, but it was released later. That movie, *Punchline*, was riskier than anything he had done so far. Hanks had built a reputation in the movie business as someone who plays likable characters. Steven Gold, his character in *Punchline*, is not likable. He is a selfish, mean-spirited comedian. He has been kicked out of medical school and locked out of his apartment because he did not pay the rent.

Hanks explained why he wanted the role of Steven Gold. "It was a well-written character, and that's all you really look for," he said. "It doesn't matter if he is hard to like. He *is* hard to like, but he is still somewhat sympathetic. You are still rooting for him in some ways."[14]

Hanks, who thinks of himself as an actor rather than a comedian, had never done stand-up comedy. The thought of getting up before a live audience to do comedy terrified him. Hanks decided to give himself a crash course in stand-up comedy before filming for *Punchline* began.

Hanks and two of his friends, who were comedians, wrote the comedy routines that he used in the movie. Then Hanks tried them out by performing live in clubs. It was not easy. "I was really bad. I was terrible," he said. "But every journey starts with the first step. I just had to go up and start being bad, so that eventually I could get comfortable enough with the horrifying prospect of getting up in front of people."[15]

Hanks's costar in *Punchline* was Sally Field. She plays Lilah Krystick, a housewife who seeks Gold's help in becoming a comedian. She also tried out her comedy routines in front of live audiences. (Hanks and Field would work together again when she was cast as his mother in *Forrest Gump*.)

Hanks said that he identified with the character of Steven Gold, noting that they had some bad characteristics in common. The character in *Punchline* had trouble balancing his work life with his personal life. "I've certainly had those problems; I think any actor has: The only time you really feel alive is when you're working," Hanks said.[16]

However, most people did not believe that Hanks could have anything in common with someone like Steven Gold. They said that Hanks was just too nice. "Nice" is a label that Hanks has learned to live with, but he does not like it much. "I'm stuck with that 'nice' thing," he said. "I'm probably as nice as the next guy, but, you know, I have my moments. It can be a pain with people having that expectation."[17]

Hanks has also said that reporters mistake his being nice with the fact that he just does not get concerned about some things. He is willing to grant interviews to reporters because there is no reason for him not to. He causes no problems at photo shoots, and follows directions on what to wear and how to look. Not cooperating is just too much trouble. "Life's too short to worry about all that," he said.[18]

On the other hand, there are two topics that Hanks will not discuss with reporters. One is his home. No reporter has ever visited his home. He also refuses to discuss his divorce from Samantha Lewes. He dismisses questions about his first marriage with generalities—they married young, and he spent too much time working instead of with his family. "I really shouldn't answer questions about the woman I married," he told one reporter.[19]

Once when he was asked about his current relationship with his former wife, Hanks said that they did not talk much. "I wouldn't say we were friends, or even friendly. But we're very respectful of each other's place and position," he explained, and he described Lewes as a good mother.[20] His children lived with their mother in Sacramento, but Hanks saw them as often as possible. In the summers, they spent long vacations with him and sometimes traveled with him when he was filming on location.

*Punchline* did not enjoy the box office success of *Big*, but critics praised Hanks for his work as Steven Gold. By the end of the year, people were predicting that Hanks would be nominated for an Oscar as Best Actor for his performance in one of those movies.

# Into the Bonfire

Comedies rarely win Oscar awards, but in February 1989, Hanks received a nomination as Best Actor for his role in *Big*. He discovered that being nominated was not entirely a good experience. "I remember standing in the auditorium where the Academy Awards were held and these guys were stickin' mikes at me, saying, 'You're not gonna win.'"[1] Their predictions were right. Dustin Hoffman won the award for Best Actor that year for his role in *Rain Man*.

Although Hanks did not win the Oscar, his popularity continued to grow. That was reflected in his salary. Hanks had gone from making $1 million per movie to a reported $3.5 million per movie. The money was not important to him. "The biggest thing about having money is not having to worry about the car," he joked. "If mine breaks down, I can have it fixed."[2]

He had also signed a development contract with Walt Disney Studios. It was similar to the working relationship that he had earlier with Columbia Pictures. As part of the new deal, he had an office at the Disney studios in Burbank, California.

Hanks did not take success too seriously. Perhaps as a reminder that success could be fleeting, he framed a fan letter and hung it in his office. The letter congratulated Hanks on his marriage and praised him for his work in *Top Gun*. Of course, Hanks was not in *Top Gun*. Tom Cruise stars in that movie.

As for his future plans, Hanks said that he did not set goals. "I've never been a goal-oriented guy," he told a reporter. "I'll wait and see what happens."[3]

In another interview, he did list some goals. "I would like to know how to surf. I would like to ride a raft down some long river. I would love to drive cross-country a few times. I would love to speak French and play the piano," he said.[4] He has accomplished at least one of those goals. Rita Wilson gave him a surfboard for his thirty-second birthday and Hanks learned to surf.

It seemed that Hanks had personal goals, but not professional ones. When selecting movie roles, his main priority was variety. "The challenge of this job is finding things you haven't done before," he said. "There's no fun and no future in doing the same thing over again."[5]

On the other hand, he felt some responsibility to

his fans to consider the type of material available to movie audiences. "There's no reason for me to play a psycho killer who butchers people with razor-sharp hubcaps," he noted.[6]

After the success of *Big* and the Oscar nomination, people flocked to the theater to see Hanks's next movie, *The 'Burbs*. In that film, described as a horror comedy, Hanks plays Ray Peterson, a man who spends his vacation at home spying on his strange neighbors. Carrie Fisher, who starred with Hanks in *The Man with One Red Shoe*, plays his suburban wife, Carol.

The first weekend was successful at the box office, but then the word got out—*The 'Burbs* was not a good movie. Ticket sales dropped off rapidly. Hanks called the movie "one of the worst films of my career."[7] He blamed the failure partly on a writers' strike that had prevented needed changes from being made to the script.

His next movie, *Turner & Hooch*, was his first film made under his development deal with Disney. It also suffered from production problems. The director, Henry Winkler, a former *Happy Days* star, was replaced twelve days after shooting began. A reporter for the *Boston Herald* wrote that the change was "allegedly because of difficulties with Hanks."[8]

Although Hanks did not say that he had a problem with Winkler, he indicated that he was not happy with the way the movie was coming together. "We shot for two weeks and there was nothing worthwhile on the screen," he said.[9] Roger Spottiswoode took over as director, but by that time they had fallen behind schedule. They rushed to catch up, which Hanks said affected the final product.

Hanks plays Scott Turner, a small-town detective bored with his job. He is about to take a position with the San Francisco Police Department when a murder takes place in town. The only witness to the crime is Hooch, a big ugly dog. A reluctant Turner is forced to work with the dog to solve the murder.

The movie enjoyed some box office success, but critics said that Hanks did a good job in a so-so movie. In *The New York Times*, Caryn James wrote, "Mr. Hanks is a brilliant understated comedian, who rises to the level of his best material, as he did in *Big*, and who has the intelligence and charm to rise above his weaker roles. He is the best part of this film."[10]

Hanks's next film, *Joe Versus the Volcano*, opened in March 1990. Hanks plays Joe Banks, who is a hypochondriac—someone who imagines he has all sorts of illnesses. Joe is told that he has a "brain cloud" and only six months to live. A billionaire promises to make those six months an adventure. In return, at the end of the six months, Joe must agree to be a human sacrifice to a Polynesian island volcano. Meg Ryan costars with Hanks, playing three different roles as the billionaire's three daughters.

This unusual movie fit in with Hanks's desire to play a variety of roles. Still, he was not sure people would like it. "It is a very weird movie and a very dangerous movie, because it was going to have to be well made in order to work. But I liked the emotional journey that Joe Banks was on," he said.[11] Unfortunately, moviegoers did not get as caught up in that journey.

*In* Turner & Hooch, *Hanks plays a policeman who teams up with an ugly pooch to solve a murder.*

The movie was another disappointment at the box office.

When *Joe Versus the Volcano* opened, Hanks was about to begin shooting for his next film, *Bonfire of the Vanities*. The movie is based on a best-selling novel by Tom Wolfe. Because the book had been so successful, early predictions were that it would be one of the biggest movies of the year. Brian DePalma was selected to direct. For months, people wondered who would be cast in the lead role of Sherman McCoy, a snobbish Wall Street bond trader.

When Tom Hanks's name was announced, there were rumblings about miscasting. People who had read the book said that he was not right for the part. "I had people on a plane just leaning over and examining me and saying, 'No, I don't see it, I just don't see it,'" Hanks recalled.[12]

Hanks, too, realized that he might not be the right actor. But he could not turn down the chance to play the lead in what was expected to be the movie of the year. "I wasn't about to say, well, gee, I can't do the role," he said.[13] After all, he was an actor, which meant that he was capable of playing a character not like himself.

In the movie, McCoy is involved with Maria Ruskin, played by Melanie Griffith. In an early scene, Ruskin is driving McCoy's Mercedes. She and McCoy feel threatened by two black youths, and she backs up into one of them. Ruskin convinces McCoy not to report the incident to the police. After the young man dies at the hospital, a police investigation connects McCoy's car to the accident. Ruskin lies, saying McCoy was driving the car at the time, and he is arrested and goes on trial.

Bruce Willis plays a washed-up, alcoholic newspaper reporter, who rises to the top again in his coverage of the incident. Rita Wilson, who travels with Hanks when he is filming on location, was in the right place at the right time when the movie was being cast. She got a small part as a public relations person in the film.

Unfortunately, what was expected to be a great movie turned out to be the biggest flop of the year. *Bonfire of the Vanities* cost about $40 million to make. On opening weekend in December 1990, it brought in $3.1 million at the box office. According to a report in *The New York Times*, a movie budgeted at $40 million needed to bring in about $10 million its first weekend.[14] *Bonfire of the Vanities* did turn out to be one of the most talked about movies of the year, but only because it was so bad.

The movie was an embarrassment for Hanks, but he said he had no idea it would turn out that way. "It feels just the same when you're filming a hit or a flop," he said. "'Bonfires' felt great when we were filming it. On the other hand, who would have thought audiences would break into applause at me dancing on a big piano keyboard in *Big*? You never know what will hit."[15]

After *Bonfire of the Vanities*, Hanks took a nineteen-month break from filmmaking. "It was the best thing for everybody," he said. "I needed a break from the industry. And the industry needed a little less of me for a while."[16]

He had made fourteen movies in six years, and he knew it was too many. "I had a body of work that was pretty hit or miss. It became a matter of just getting it done, as opposed to doing it right, so I had to pull back," he said.[17]

The break gave him a chance to enjoy surfing, skiing, and doing things with his family. In 1990, he and Rita Wilson had a son, Chester. Hanks also spent time with his father, who was seriously ill with the kidney disease that had plagued him much of his life. Amos Hanks died in 1992.

During the break, Hanks signed up with a different talent agency. Some people said that *Bonfire of the Vanities* was the reason behind the change, but Hanks disagreed. It was something that had been in the works for quite some time. After working with the same agency for twelve years, Hanks said leaving was a lot like getting a divorce. It was a painful decision, and like his divorce, it was something that he did not want to discuss with reporters.

In 1992, Hanks made a brief appearance in *Radio Flyer*. The movie stars Elijah Wood and Joseph Mazzello as two young brothers, Mike and Bobby. Their stepfather physically abuses Bobby, and Mike tries to help his brother. The film's title comes from the flying machine that the boys build from a Radio Flyer red wagon and other parts that they find around their home.

Hanks is on-screen for only a few minutes. He appears at the beginning and at the end of the movie as a grown-up Mike telling his own children what happened to their Uncle Bobby. Offscreen, he serves as the narrator of the story. Hanks insisted on being unbilled—not named in the movie credits. This meant that his name could not be used in any advertising for the film.

Hanks's real return to the screen was in a surprising role in *A League of Their Own*, released in the summer of 1992. The movie is about the All-American Girls Professional Baseball League (AAGPBL), teams that played for a brief time during World War II. At that time, most men, including many baseball players, were being called to serve in the armed forces during the war. As a result, organized baseball suffered. The game that many referred to as "America's favorite sport" was losing fans. To keep Americans interested in the sport, the AAGPBL was formed.

Hanks actively pursued the part of Jimmy Dugan, the alcoholic, washed-up Major League ballplayer who coaches the team. Penny Marshall, the director of *Big*, also directed *A League of Their Own*. She did not think that Hanks was right for the part. Marshall said that Hanks told her he could do it and that he needed the job. "I just did five pictures that tanked!" he said.[18]

Hanks gained thirty pounds for the role, a goal that he says he accomplished with frequent trips to Dairy Queen. "The reason I got as heavy as I did was to give the audience a sense that this guy, when he was in shape, had really been an athlete," Hanks explained.[19] Hanks also thought that there had to be a reason that Dugan was coaching an all-girl baseball league instead of fighting for his country. He suggested to Marshall that Dugan have an injury that would

*"There's no crying in baseball!" Coach Jimmy Dugan (Tom Hanks) scolds one of his ballplayers (Bitty Schram) in* A League of Their Own.

keep him out of the war. Thus, Dugan walked with a limp.

This was a supporting role for Hanks. The stars of the movie were the actresses who played ballplayers on the team, including Geena Davis, Madonna, and Rosie O'Donnell. But Hanks liked what the film did for his career. "It was brand new turf for me," he said, "because it wasn't the romantic lead of the movie. I was the big fat guy in the back, which actually was a blast to do. And it opened up a lot of avenues for me."[20]

It showed directors that Hanks did not have to be

the star and that he was willing to play an unattractive character. "That's a marvelous message to put out there," Hanks noted.[21] *A League of Their Own* was another turning point in Hanks's career, the beginning of what he called his "modern era of moviemaking."[22] In that new era, he did a much better job of selecting movie roles for himself, taking on "meatier," more serious roles.

# Taking a Risk

Hanks had another success to his credit, but he did not forget where he got his start. In March 1993, he returned to Great Lakes Theater Festival near Cleveland to star in eleven fund-raising performances of a play titled *Now Playing Center*.

In June 1993, his next movie, *Sleepless in Seattle*, opened. Hanks plays Sam Baldwin, a widower who moves from Chicago to Seattle. He hopes that the change of scenery will help him cope with his wife's death. But he is still lonely, and his eight-year-old son, Jonah, tries to help. During the holiday season, Jonah hears the host of a national radio show invite listeners to call in with their Christmas wishes. Jonah's wish is that his dad will find a new wife and stop being so sad. The radio host talks Jonah into putting his dad on the phone to tell his story.

Meg Ryan costars as Annie Reed, one of the thousands of women who hear Sam on the radio and are touched by what he has to say. They write to him, hoping for a chance to meet him. Sam ignores the letters, but Jonah reads them and picks Annie as right for Sam. The hard part is persuading his dad to meet her.

It was the second movie that Ryan and Hanks starred in together. The first was the ill-fated *Joe Versus the Volcano*. However, they did not spend a lot of time working together for *Sleepless*. Throughout most of the movie, their characters are on opposite coasts of the United States. Most of their scenes were filmed separately.

In the movie, Annie writes to Sam, suggesting that they meet at the top of the Empire State Building. It is a scene stolen from the 1957 movie *An Affair to Remember*, starring Cary Grant and Deborah Kerr. Sam is not familiar with that movie, so his friend Suzy gives him a brief summary of the plot. Rita Wilson plays Suzy. It was not a large part, but she got a lot of attention for her crying in that scene.

Wilson is a talented actress, but she has not enjoyed the same level of success as her husband. That is partly because she has made her family her first priority. Wilson plans her acting jobs around Hanks's career so that the family can travel together when Hanks films on location. Some people have wondered whether Wilson felt cheated somehow. Was she envious of her husband's career? a reporter asked.

Eight-year-old Jonah (Ross Malinger) hopes his widowed father (Hanks) will find love and happiness with Annie (Meg Ryan) in the romantic comedy Sleepless in Seattle.

"Oh, people have always thought that about me," Wilson said. "But why would they think there would be any kind of competition between two people who have a healthy relationship? And who's to say my career would be any different if I weren't married to Tom?"[1]

Hanks had turned down the role of Sam Baldwin the first time he was offered the part. In the first version of the script, Hanks thought Sam was too weak. He accepted the role after director Nora Ephron and her sister Delia Ephron rewrote the script. However, Hanks and Nora Ephron still had disagreements about his character. Hanks felt a responsibility to present the man's point of view. "I gave her a bunch of grief," Hanks said. "Mostly about my character's relationship with his son. She had written it more like a mother-son relationship."[2]

Hanks said that their different points of view made the movie better, and Nora Ephron agreed. She said that Hanks "basically rewrites every part he plays."[3] However, it did not cause any problems on the set of *Sleepless in Seattle* because he made his suggestions in a good way. "He sits with the director and the writer and says: 'Wouldn't it be nice if this happened?' Or 'Why doesn't he say this?'" Ephron explained.[4]

Some say that it is Hanks's ability to edit a script that has made him so successful as an actor. "He is completely brilliant, a force on a screenplay," said one producer who worked with Hanks. "He knows how to sharpen lines and scenes, especially for himself, and he brings the whole thing up a level."[5]

Another reason for his success, according to Nora Ephron, is that he is able to act on so many different levels. When he is playing a funny scene, he might also add sadness and anger. *Sleepless in Seattle* was billed as a romantic comedy, but what Hanks also brought to that movie was the sadness of a man grieving the loss of his wife.

*Sleepless in Seattle* was a big summer hit in 1993, holding its own against *Jurassic Park*, which was released at the same time. Although critics thought the movie was too cute, there was no denying the appeal of Tom Hanks and Meg Ryan. They have become one of the best-loved on-screen couples.

In his next film, *Philadelphia*, Hanks took a very

serious role as Andrew Beckett, a gay lawyer who loses his job after his employers learn that he has AIDS. Beckett files a discrimination suit against his former law firm. Denzel Washington plays Joe Miller, a lawyer who agrees to represent Beckett in the case. Miller is homophobic—he hates people who are gay.

There had been other movies about AIDS, but this was the first big-budget movie on the subject. Hanks would be the first box office star to play a gay man. Some people wondered if Hanks was taking too big a chance, and they predicted that such a controversial part could ruin his career. But Hanks thought it was a great part and he wanted a chance to work with director Jonathan Demme. Demme had recently achieved success directing *The Silence of the Lambs*, starring Jodie Foster and Anthony Hopkins.

Hanks did a lot of research to prepare himself. He read books about AIDS and talked to doctors. After gathering background information, he spent time at the Philadelphia AIDS Institute, talking to men who had the disease. He asked them hard questions such as how they felt when they learned they had AIDS. The people he talked to were very honest in their replies, which helped him understand his character better.

During filming, Hanks lost thirty pounds and had his head shaved to give the appearance of someone whose body was wasting away with the disease. The dieting was done under a doctor's care. "They put me on a diet, with lunch that would fit in a teacup and the dinner on a saucer," Hanks recalled.[6]

By the end of filming, Hanks looked so sickly that

he could barely stand to look at himself in a mirror. He could not overlook the irony of his situation. "I kept thinking, 'Here I am working at this and there are millions of people who can't stop it from happening,'" he said.[7]

Hanks was concerned about AIDS, but he did not take the role to make a political statement. Although many actors use their influence to support political causes, Hanks keeps his political thoughts to himself. "I don't feel that anybody is influenced in any way by the fact that a public figure on the show-business level embraces any sort of political cause," he said.[8]

On the other hand, the part did give him an opportunity to spend some time at the White House. After a private screening of the movie, President Clinton invited Hanks and Rita Wilson to stay overnight at the White House. "It was a *huge* thrill," Hanks said, "a very prestigious bed and breakfast."[9] He had a hard time sleeping that night—he was just too excited about being there.

*Philadelphia* was released in December 1993. According to film critic Roger Ebert, it had been scheduled to be released earlier in the year. But it was held until the holiday season because those working on the film felt that it had Oscar potential. "The holidays are known in the business as the Oscar Season," Ebert explained.[10]

Hanks received his second Oscar nomination as Best Actor for his role as Andrew Beckett. He flew his mother in for the awards ceremony in March 1994. When Hanks was announced as the winner, she cried. "It was one of the happiest moments of my life," she said.[11]

Hanks was also filled with emotion. During his acceptance speech, he fought back tears as he talked about how happy he was that his family was with him to share that moment. He also paid tribute to those who had died from AIDS. "My work is magnified by the fact that the streets of heaven are too crowded with angels—we know their names. They number a thousand for each of the red ribbons [AIDS awareness ribbons] we wear here tonight."[12] He also thanked two gay men who had influenced his life: Rawley Farnsworth, his high school drama teacher, and John Gilkerson, a friend from high school.

The audience at the awards ceremony gave Hanks a standing ovation. However, in newspapers the next day reporters called his speech strange. They said he had rambled on, not making much sense. John Gilkerson had died of AIDS in 1989, but how did Farnsworth feel about Hank's statement? Hanks revealed that Farnsworth was gay in front of millions of people watching the televised awards program. For the next few months, in almost every interview, Hanks had to answer reporters' questions about that speech.

"The reason I was standing there was because so many gay men have died of AIDS," Hanks told one reporter.[13] He said that he felt he needed to address that issue in his speech. As for his former teacher, Hanks had talked to Farnsworth in advance about what he intended to say. Farnsworth, who had retired from teaching, gave Hanks his approval.

*Hanks is proud of winning the Academy Award for Best Actor for his role in* Philadelphia. *In the film, he stars as a gay lawyer dying of AIDS.*

Hanks said that if he rambled in his speech, it was because it was hard to remember what he wanted to say in the excitement of the moment. "It's like your head fills up with a river of plasma. Your heart suddenly pumps at such a horrible rate that you think it's going to burst out of your chest," he noted.[14]

Hanks did not mind that people criticized his speech. He said that it was part of the fun of the Academy Awards. He recalled that he had done the same thing himself to past winners. "I can tell you right now, whatever you say in your speech, it's really cool to be up there," he said.[15]

With that Oscar, Hanks became the first actor to go from starring on a television sitcom to winning an Oscar. Sally Field, Hanks's costar in *Punchline*, was the first actress to achieve that honor. She had once been known as the flying nun on a television series with that name. She went on to win two Oscars for Best Actress, one in 1979 for her role in the movie *Norma Rae* and one in 1984 for *Places in the Heart*. Field and Hanks teamed up again in Hanks's next movie, *Forrest Gump*. In that movie, Field plays his mother.

# Journey into Space

$H$anks took another risk with *Forrest Gump*, released in July 1994. Would moviegoers be interested in the story of a man with a low IQ who has a series of unbelievable adventures? Hanks gambled that they would. "When I read the script for *Gump*, I saw it as one of those kind of grand, hopeful movies that the audience can go to and feel exactly that: some hope for their lot and their position in life," he said.[1]

Hank's only concern was that he needed to speak with a southern accent. "I was afraid of any sort of dialect," he said.[2] He managed the accent by adopting the style of Michael Humphrey, the eight-year-old Mississippi boy cast in the movie as the young Forrest Gump.

Running is a recurring theme in the movie. It is the reason for much of Gump's success. But Hanks did not actually run in many of those scenes. "Doubles" who look like the star often do the movie stunts or appear in scenes that do not show the star's face. Hanks's younger brother, Jim Hanks, who is also an actor, doubled for his brother. Jim Hanks was the only one who could duplicate his brother's stiff-legged running stride. "Tom had other doubles, but they couldn't do the run," Jim Hanks explained. "That's a stupid Hanks thing."[3]

Tom Hanks takes his job seriously, but he also has fun when he is working and he can be a bit unpredictable. Mykelti Williamson, who stars as Gump's friend Bubba, gave an example of Hanks's ability to surprise people. One day, when they were filming on location in South Carolina, Williamson and Hanks drove past a church where a wedding party was standing outside. "Tom jumped out of the car, kissed both the bride and the groom, and then jumped back in and we left," Williamson said.[4] The shocked couple was left wondering if it was really Tom Hanks.

Hanks believed so strongly in *Forrest Gump* that he took a lower salary in exchange for a share of the profits. His gamble paid off. *Forrest Gump* was a huge hit and Hanks's share of the earnings was reportedly $40 million.

In spite of his wealth, Hanks lives simply by Hollywood standards. "I try to live as modestly as I can for someone with too many houses," he said.[5] "Too many" in his case is three—a home in Los

Angeles, a beach home in Malibu, and a place in New York City.

In a business where an actor is only as good as his last movie, Hanks was doing very well. He had four hits in a row—*A League of Their Own*, *Sleepless in Seattle*, *Philadelphia*, and *Forrest Gump*. The success of *Forrest Gump* coming on the tail of an Oscar for *Philadelphia* was beyond anything that Hanks could imagine. "It's an embarrassment of riches," he said. "I mean, you can't plan on this, and you can't desire it too much. You can only sort of let it wash over you and say, 'Man, oh, man! How'd that happen? Who was that guy?'"[6]

In March 1995, Hanks won his second Oscar for Best Actor for his role in *Forrest Gump*. During his acceptance speech, he paid tribute to his wife. "I'm standing here because the woman I share my life with has taught me and demonstrates to me every day just what love is," he said.[7]

Friends say that Hanks's marriage to Wilson has changed him. She has given him the family stability that he longed for as a child. Her family members are close, and they see or talk to one another almost daily. Wilson's mother is their nanny. Her brother, a professional cook, sometimes prepares dinner for the family, and her sister visits often. Hanks enjoys this extended family. "Just being part of a big family means there's always something to do," he said.[8]

Hanks says that his marriage to Wilson has helped his career. "I belong to a home—it's a rock, it's steady. Which means that my mind is freed up to do a whole different kind of work," he said.[9]

*"The woman I share my life with has taught me and demonstrates to me every day just what love is," says Hanks of his wife, Rita Wilson.*

Hanks was glad that he had already signed on for his next movie before he knew how big *Gump* would be. Otherwise, in deciding on his next role, he might have focused only on topping *Gump*. He prefers not to think too much in choosing his roles. "It has to be a purely emotional and instinctive choice: because you love the material and you want to tell the story," he said.[10] On an emotional level, his next role was perfect. Hanks, who was fascinated with space travel as a teenager, was about to journey into space in *Apollo 13*.

The movie tells the story of the ill-fated *Apollo 13* moon mission in April 1970. Two days into the flight, an oxygen tank exploded in the command module, the main part of the spacecraft. The three astronauts on board were two hundred thousand miles from home. With their oxygen supply seeping out of the spacecraft, they climbed into the lunar module for safety.

The lunar module was the small vehicle used to actually land on the moon. It was designed to carry two astronauts and had oxygen and food supplies to keep two astronauts alive for two days. Now three astronauts were depending on those supplies and it would take four days to bring them home.

Hanks was thirteen years old when the *Apollo 13* spaceflight took place. He raced home after school to get reports on the fate of the astronauts. Commander Jim Lovell was Hanks's hero. Now Hanks would portray Lovell in the movie.

As part of his preparation, Hanks spent four days at Lovell's home. He asked Lovell questions about spaceflight, and Lovell took Hanks flying in his plane.

"I did some test-pilot stunts and let him fly the plane," Lovell recalled. "He made a great pilot."[11]

During that time, Hanks, who is a great observer, even learned how to act like Lovell. "He perfectly imitated Lovell's flat astronaut voice and the way he walked across a room, bent slightly forward, as if nothing was going to get in his way," a writer for *Texas Monthly* noted.[12]

Hanks also studied the transcripts of the *Apollo 13* mission. The transcripts recorded the actual conversations between the astronauts and Mission Control during the flight. Hanks wanted to get a feel for the language they used.

Director Ron Howard appreciated Hanks's attention to detail. Hanks and Howard had become friends on the set of *Splash*. Howard was happy to be working with Hanks again. "I call him the no muss, no fuss superstar," Howard said.[13]

Howard also noted how much Hanks had matured as an actor. During the filming of *Splash*, Howard spent a lot of time telling Hanks what to do. Howard's role as director had changed with *Apollo 13*. "My job with Tom on this one is just to kind of stay out of the way. He's great. He's in such a groove. It's a hundred and eighty degrees from *Splash*," Howard said.[14]

Howard wanted to make the movie as realistic as possible. He started by sending the actors to space camp for a month. There they flew missions in a NASA simulator. A simulator looks like the actual vehicle that is used in a spaceflight except that it never leaves the ground.

The scenes with the astronauts floating in the

weightlessness of space were actually filmed in weightless conditions aboard NASA's training jet, the KC-135. The jet, nicknamed the "Vomit Comit," has a stripped-down cargo area with padded walls. The pilot flies arcs called parabolas. At the top of the arc, the pilot turns and makes a sharp dive. The passengers are weightless for about thirty seconds.

Learning the tricks of moving around in weightless conditions took practice. "There were times when we'd finish shooting a scene, and I had no idea which way I was going to fall," Hanks said.[15] But he enjoyed the feeling of weightlessness. "It's not a sensation you can liken to anything else," he noted. "It's not floating like superman but kind of floating like an angel."[16]

During the actual *Apollo 13* flight, the astronauts shut down the power on the spacecraft. They wanted to conserve energy because they would need it later to reenter the earth's atmosphere. With no power, temperatures quickly dropped inside the lunar module. In order to recreate those conditions for the movie, Howard brought in large refrigeration units that cooled the set to thirty-four degrees Fahrenheit, only two degrees above freezing. The crew spent five weeks filming in the cold temperatures, but no amount of discomfort could dampen Hanks's joy in living the life of an astronaut. "If they said, 'You can go on the shuttle, but you'll have to give away two years to train, study and prepare,' I'd gladly do it," Hanks said.[17]

*Apollo 13* pulled in more than $172 million at the box office. It was also a hit with critics, who praised Hanks's portrayal of Lovell. "His Lovell—as strong, faithful and emotionally straightforward as Forrest

*Tom Hanks, Bill Paxton (center), and Kevin Bacon in a scene from Apollo 13. The movie recreated the excitement and tension of the ill-fated 1970 mission to the moon.*

Gump—carries the story like a precious oxygen back-pack," wrote Richard Corliss in *Time* magazine.[18]

Some thought that Hanks might win an Oscar for Best Actor for the third year in a row, something that no actor had ever done. That never happened, but Hanks did not appear to be concerned. In a television skit on *Saturday Night Live*, he poked fun at himself, playing an actor who whined because he did not win his third Oscar.

Hanks moved behind the scenes for *Toy Story*, the first computer-animated full-length film. *Toy Story* is about the toys belonging to a boy named Andy. When Andy is not around, his toys come to life. Hanks provides the voice of Sheriff Woody, a pull-string cowboy. Woody is Andy's favorite toy and the leader of the other toys. His position is challenged by the arrival of Buzz Lightyear, a battery-operated spaceman. Actor-comedian Tim Allen is the voice of Lightyear.

John Lasseter, a former animator for Disney, was the director. (Later, in 1998, he went on to direct *A Bug's Life*.) Hanks was Lasseter's first choice for the role of Woody. The next step was persuading Hanks to do it. Lasseter put together a thirty-second film clip of the computer-animated Woody combined with Hanks's voice from *Turner & Hooch*. When Hanks saw it, his only question was "When can we start?"[19]

Hanks was paid only a little more than union scale (the minimum) for *Toy Story*. He worked on the movie over a two-year period, going back to re-record dialogue each time changes were made in the script. Hanks said that it was hard work. Usually when he was filming a movie, he would do a scene and then have time to rest while the crew set up the next scene. He did not have those breaks with *Toy Story*. "You have to essentially act full-bore 100 percent, standing there with your headphones on for three or four hours at a time," Hanks said.[20]

No one knew how the public would react to the first computer-animated feature film. *Toy Story* opened on November 22, 1995, without a lot of advance publicity. To almost everyone's surprise, it earned more than $38 million at the box office on opening weekend. In *Time* magazine, critic Richard Corliss called it "the year's most inventive comedy" and praised Sheriff Woody as "wonderfully voiced by Tom Hanks."[21]

The following month, December 1995, Hanks and Rita Wilson celebrated the birth of their second son. They decided to name him Truman Theodore after two presidents—Harry S. Truman and Theodore Roosevelt.

At that time, Hanks was busy with *That Thing You Do*, working behind the scenes as both writer and director. Hanks had already tried directing on a smaller scale, doing three television shows—one episode each of HBO's *Tales of the Crypt* (1992), *Fallen Angels* (1993), and *A League of Their Own* (1993)—a short-lived television series based on the movie. However, *That Thing You Do* was his first attempt to direct a full-length movie, and it was also his first experience writing a screenplay.

# From Star to Superstar

$H$anks had begun thinking about *That Thing You Do* during a publicity tour for *Forrest Gump*. He was hot—it seemed that everyone was interested in Tom Hanks. Reporters wanted to interview him and people were talking about his Oscar-quality performance in *Forrest Gump*. Hanks needed to get his mind off all the craziness that came with the success of *Gump*. "It's a time when all you're doing is talking about yourself, and that's a very unhealthy thing to do," Hanks said. "Not only that, it's not very enjoyable."[1]

So he began writing a script. When it was finished he took the script to 20th Century-Fox. In 1993, Hanks had ended his working relationship with Disney Studios. The following year, he reached a development agreement with Fox. The studio agreed to produce his new film as long as the budget was kept at a "moderate" level.

Of course, part of the reason that Fox agreed to do the movie could have been that his name was Tom Hanks. After a string of successful films, Hanks had risen from star to superstar status. With that came a certain amount of power. "The good thing about that is that I'm getting to see a lot of scripts first, and I understand that my participation can start a film project, which is nice," Hanks said.[2]

His name opened doors, but he still had to prove that he could do the job. "If my name had been Tom Smith, they [Fox] might not have read it. But if it goes smackeroo, flop, you won't see me directing anything else. You don't get a second chance," Hanks said.[3]

*That Thing You Do* is a story about a year in the life of a garage band called the Wonders. During that year, they enjoy a quick rise to the top of the music charts and begin a national tour on the basis of one hit. As their popularity climbs, the band starts to crumble.

The film is set in 1964, when the music world was caught up in the midst of the "British Invasion." At that time, British groups such as the Beatles, the Dave Clark Five, and Gerry and the Pacemakers were topping the music charts. Thousands of screaming fans flocked to their concerts. Hanks was eight years old in 1964, but with an older brother and sister in the house, he was very aware of the British Invasion and its effects. Although the Beatles were the most popular of the groups, Hanks's favorite was the Dave Clark Five.

Hanks chose not to use any actual songs from the sixties in the movie. "All those great '60s hits are everywhere in films and commercials. I wanted something new," he said.[4] The title song, "That Thing You Do," was selected through a contest. Hanks reviewed almost three hundred songs submitted on tape. Adam Schlesinger, a twenty-eight-year-old songwriter from New York, won the contest. All the other songs in the movie were also written to sound like music from the '60s. Hanks wrote four of them himself.

For Hanks, directing a movie was a big change from starring in one. As an actor, he could go home and relax after a day of shooting. As a director, he still had to look over rushes—film shot that day—and prepare for the next day's problems. Hanks said that directing changed him as an actor, because it made him more sympathetic to what the director does. "You [an actor] may get bored sitting in your trailer, but the director never gets to go to the trailer," Hanks explained. "For this job, I started at 4 A.M. every day and didn't get home until 11:45 at night."[5]

On the other hand, Hanks had a good time casting friends and family in the movie. Peter Scolari had a small part as the host of "The Hollywood Television Showcase." Ron Howard's brother, Clint, and Penny Marshall's daughter, Tracy Reiner, were also in the movie. Hanks cast his wife, Rita Wilson, as a cocktail waitress. Hanks's children from his first marriage, Colin and Elizabeth, had small nonspeaking roles.

*Hanks wrote a script about a fictional band that achieves national fame in the 1960s. Then he stepped behind the camera to direct the movie—*That Thing You Do.

"Otherwise I don't see them," he joked. "So I'll make them work so I can spend time with them."[6]

Hanks also had a small part as Mr. White, the record executive who molds the band into a success. However, when success begins to affect the personal lives of the band members, it is not clear whether Mr. White has helped them or hurt them. Hanks said he wrote the part of Mr. White for himself because "I rarely get to be the mysterious guy in the back with questionable motivations. You know: 'Is he a good guy? Is he a bad guy? What's with the dude?'"[7]

For the band members, Hanks cast four actors

who were not very well known—Johnathon Schaech, Steve Zahn, Ethan Embry, and Tom Everett Scott. It was the first movie role for Scott, who plays the drummer and bandleader, but not his first role with national exposure. He had appeared a number of times on the television series *Grace Under Fire*.

Scott's casting was notable because he looked a lot like a young Tom Hanks. In fact, Hanks at first hesitated about casting Scott, concerned that "it's just gonna be too odd."[8] Then he realized that the resemblance could work to his advantage. It was believable that White would help a young man who reminded him so much of himself.

Although Hanks later said that there were things about the movie he would like to change, he was satisfied with his debut as director. He actually enjoyed watching it. "I thought that when it came down to the public seeing it for the first time, I'd be in the back of the car throwing up on the way to the cinema. But I can't wait to get there. So, call me a goof," he said.[9]

Reviews of the movie were mixed. Some said that it did not have much of a plot, but most agreed that Hanks had succeeded in making a movie that was fun to watch. In *People* magazine, Leah Rozen called it "a pleasingly bouncy movie."[10]

In the meantime, Hanks was preparing to take another trip into space and to add a new title to his résumé—executive producer. In 1997, he produced a twelve-part HBO miniseries, *From the Earth to the Moon*. The series, based on Andrew Chaikin's book *A Man on the Moon*, covered the entire Apollo project.

This was the U.S. space program that put a man on the moon. Chaikin was a consultant for the series.

The $68 million series was the most expensive original programming in HBO's history. As executive producer, Hanks was in charge. He did the budgeting, saw the script through to completion, and hired key people—the production staff, ten directors, twelve writers, and numerous actors. In most miniseries, each show is a continuation of the one before it. But in this series every segment could stand on its own. Each show had its own director. Hanks directed the first segment and wrote the last one. He also had a hand in writing other segments, and he hosted the series, introducing each of the shows.

As had become his custom, Hanks called on friends and family to work on the project. He had three coproducers for the series—Ron Howard, Howard's partner Brian Grazer, and Michael Bostwick. The three had worked together on *Apollo 13*. One of the directors was Hanks's friend Sally Field, who directed a segment on the wives of the astronauts. Peter Scolari plays astronaut Pete Conrad in the first show, and Hanks's wife, Rita Wilson, plays Susan Borman, the wife of astronaut Frank Borman.

The miniseries began airing on Sunday evening, April 5, 1998. Two episodes were shown back-to-back over a period of six consecutive Sundays. The series was awarded "Program of the Year" honors by the Television Critics Association and won an Emmy award for Outstanding Miniseries.

In 1998, Hanks starred in Steven Spielberg's World War II movie, *Saving Private Ryan*. In the film, military leaders discover that three Ryan brothers have been killed in action—and they make it a mission to find Mrs. Ryan's only remaining son and bring him home. Hanks plays Captain John Miller, who is in charge of the small group of soldiers that goes behind enemy lines to find Private Ryan, played by Matt Damon.

Hanks and Spielberg had been good friends for years. In fact, Hanks lives just down the road from Spielberg. Kate Capshaw, Spielberg's wife, is one of Rita Wilson's best friends. However, Hanks and Spielberg did not purposely plan to work together on *Private Ryan*. That came about almost accidentally, when producer Mark Gordon sent both of them copies of the script at the same time. They each decided to do the movie before finding out that the other had read the script and was interested, too.

To prepare for the role, Hanks and the seven men of Captain Miller's team went to boot camp. "We hiked all over the place; it was rainy and cold and wet," Hanks recalled. "We slept on the ground and ate food that came out of cans, heated up over little tiny stoves."[11]

The actors cast as the soldiers on Miller's team became discouraged with the training and wanted to quit early. They took a vote and everyone, except Hanks, voted to go home. Spielberg later recalled the telephone call he received from Hanks telling him that they had a problem. "I said, well, look, I'm thousands of miles away. You're a filmmaker, you're a leader, solve it," Spielberg told him.[12]

Hanks told the others that they could quit, but he

*Tom Hanks and Rita Wilson are good friends with filmmaker Steven Spielberg and his wife, Kate Capshaw. Spielberg directed Hanks in* Saving Private Ryan.

was going to see it through. Then they took another vote, and this time they all voted to stay.

It seems that Hanks is very much like Captain Miller. He gives 110 percent on the job, and he expects those around him to work just as hard. His coworkers do not get angry—they know he expects no more from them than he gives himself. Like Captain Miller, he is a leader by example. Also like Captain Miller, he focuses on the work and keeps his private life to himself.

Both the Spielberg and Hanks families were on location together in England and Ireland, where they spent three months filming. Truman and Chester

Hanks, ages two and eight, ran around the trailers playing soldier with Spielberg's six-year-old son, Sawyer. But it was not child's play for Spielberg and Hanks, who were making a movie that some have called the most realistic film about World War II ever made.

*Saving Private Ryan* pulled in $190 million at the box office. Reviewers praised Hanks for his portrayal of Captain Miller. A writer for *People* magazine said that Hanks "should start making room on his mantel for a third Oscar right now."[13]

Filming *Saving Private Ryan* strongly affected Hanks. At that time, the Advertising Council was conducting a fund-raising campaign to raise money for a National World War II Memorial. Hanks volunteered his time, appearing in public service advertisements to raise public awareness and support for the memorial. "After the experience of making the film *Saving Private Ryan*, I was surprised to realize there is no national memorial to honor the men and women who served in World War II," Hanks said. "When I learned that the memorial could become a reality, I immediately wanted to be part of the effort."[14]

Once again, Hanks showed his versatility as an actor when he went from *Saving Private Ryan* to the romantic comedy *You've Got Mail*. Hanks and Meg Ryan star together again, playing a couple who get along well online—when their true identities are masked—but do not like each other in person. Nora Ephron, who had directed Ryan and Hanks five years earlier in *Sleepless in Seattle*, also directed *You've Got*

*Mail.* As with *Sleepless*, she and her sister Delia Ephron wrote the screenplay.

*You've Got Mail* is an updated version of a 1940s movie, *The Shop Around the Corner*, which starred Jimmy Stewart and Margaret Sullavan. Hanks has often been compared to Jimmy Stewart, who also starred in the holiday classic *It's a Wonderful Life*. Like Stewart, Hanks has often played ordinary guys in unusual circumstances.

In *You've Got Mail*, Hanks plays Joe Fox, a businessman who, with his family, owns a chain of bookstores. Ryan is Kathleen Kelly, the owner of a small children's bookstore that is about to be run out of business by the chain store. This, of course, leads to a bad relationship between Fox and Kelly. What they do not realize is that they are the same two people who have been happily corresponding through e-mail for some time as NY152 and Shopgirl.

*You've Got Mail* was a holiday release in December 1998. Reviewers criticized the movie, saying that it did not have much of a story, but it did well at the box office. Apparently, moviegoers were just happy to see Tom Hanks and Meg Ryan together again on-screen.

In 1999, Hanks was again nominated for an Oscar as Best Actor. This time it was for his role as Captain Miller in *Saving Private Ryan*. The award that year went to Italian actor Roberto Benigni for his role in *Life Is Beautiful*. However, Hanks would soon receive another important award.

# Honoring Hanks

On April 29, 1999, a crowd of about eight hundred people gathered at the Waldorf-Astoria Hotel in New York City, where Tom Hanks was being honored by the American Museum of the Moving Image (AMMI). It was a black-tie affair, with the men in tuxedos and women in evening gowns. Guests included Sally Field, Ron Howard, Steven Spielberg, Nora Ephron, Geena Davis, Peter Scolari, and Jim Lovell. During the two-hour program, several of the guests—Hanks's friends and coworkers—poked fun at Hanks and paid tribute to him. They talked about his career and the kind of person he is. Steven Spielberg described Hanks best when he said, "Tom is from that old-time America, when tradition and pride in your country were things you didn't scoff at."[1]

*Hanks and Wilson arrive at the American Museum of the Moving Image. Hanks was honored there in 1999 for a lifetime of achievement in the film industry.*

At forty-two, Hanks was the youngest person to be honored by the AMMI for a lifetime of achievement. But he was a long way from thinking about retirement. In 1999, Hanks was busier than ever.

He was the voice of Sheriff Woody in *Toy Story 2*, which was released in November 1999. This time Buzz Lightyear, again voiced by Tim Allen, and the other toys rescue Woody from a toy collector. Although film sequels are often disappointments, reviewers praised *Toy Story 2* even more than the widely admired original *Toy Story*.

The following month, *The Green Mile* premiered.

The movie, based on a six-part serial by horror writer Stephen King, received an Academy Award nomination for Best Picture. The setting is a Louisiana penitentiary in the 1930s. Hanks plays Paul Edgecombe, a kindhearted prison guard in the prison's death row. As prisoner John Coffey, Michael Clarke Duncan earned a nomination for Best Supporting Actor. Coffey, a black man who has been condemned for killing two white girls, has mysterious healing powers. The title of the movie comes from the green linoleum floor that leads to the prison's electric chair.

Hanks was also involved in one of the most unusual filming schedules ever for *Cast Away*. He plays a man who survives a plane crash on a deserted island. He has nothing to eat but fish and coconuts. After being marooned for four years, he is scrawny and covered with sores.

The movie is directed by Robert Zemeckis, who also directed Hanks in *Forrest Gump*. Zemeckis said that the only realistic way to film such a movie was to have Hanks actually lose enough weight to look as if he had been starving on a deserted island. Filming started in January 1999. After a couple of months, the cast and crew took a long break while Hanks dieted to lose more than fifty pounds. In April 2000, filming began for the part of the movie taking place after Hanks's character had spent months on the island.

The movie was expected to cost about $100 million to make. The biggest expense was salaries: The crew still had to be paid for all those months when there was no actual filming.

During that break, Hanks was busy behind the scenes. Continuing their interest in World War II history, Hanks and Steven Spielberg were executive producers for an HBO miniseries, *Band of Brothers*. The series began filming in England in the spring of 2000 for a 2001 debut.

Tom Hanks was not the only Hanks making news. In 1999, his son Colin was cast in *Roswell*, a new series on the WB television network. The series is based on a report of a crash of an alien spacecraft in Roswell, New Mexico, in 1947. Colin Hanks plays a human teenager who keeps the crash secret. He also had a role in *Whatever It Takes*, a romantic comedy for teens.

Hanks has not encouraged his children to follow in his footsteps as an actor. But he has not discouraged them either. He tries to keep them out of the public eye as much as possible. "It's neither wise nor is it fair to thrust them in the public eye, because they haven't made the choice," he explained.[2]

Still, he does want his children to know about his work. "All my kids can look and see what I do for a living and see that it's really fun. It produces a vast amount of joy. It's hard work if you can get it, but it's great work too," Hanks said.[3] If his children decide to become actors, they have his support and they have a fine example of what can be accomplished through hard work.

Starting out in the theater, Hanks wanted to learn everything about the business, including building sets and running the lights. In the movie business he has been just as eager to learn. He has perfected

*Hanks's son Colin launched his own acting career in 1999. Here, television actors Colin Hanks* (Roswell) *and Busy Phillips* (Freaks and Geeks) *arrive at the premiere of* The Green Mile.

his acting skills, becoming what is known in the entertainment business as a bankable star. In his column for *Parade Magazine*, Walter Scott explained what that meant. "In Hollywood, a bankable star is an actor who's paid $10 million or more per picture on the assumption that he or she can guarantee opening-weekend revenues of $25 million to $50 million at the box office."[4]

Stars do not always live up to those expectations, but since *A League of Their Own*, in 1992, Hanks's batting average has been impressive. He has also become a respected director and a powerful producer. At the same time, he remains the man you would like to have move in next door. It is that quality that makes him one of America's favorite superstars.

1956—Tom Hanks is born on July 9 in Concord, California.

1974—Graduates from Skyline High School in Oakland, California; enrolls at Chabot Community College.

1976—Transfers to California State University in Sacramento.

1977—Becomes a summer intern at Great Lakes Shakespeare Festival in Cleveland, Ohio.

1978—Receives the Cleveland Drama Critics Award; marries Samantha Lewes; son Colin is born.

1980—Has a small part in the movie *He Knows You're Alone*; premiere of the television series *Bosom Buddies*.

1981—Daughter Elizabeth is born.

1982—*Bosom Buddies* is canceled; stars in the television movie *Mazes and Monsters*.

1984—Stars in two films, *Splash* and *Bachelor Party*.

1985—Stars in *The Man with One Red Shoe* and *Volunteers*.

1986—Stars in *The Money Pit*, *Nothing in Common*, and *Every Time We Say Goodbye*.

1987—*Dragnet* is released; divorce from Samantha Lewes becomes final.

1988—Marries Rita Wilson on April 30; stars in two films, *Big* and *Punchline*.

1989—Nominated for an Oscar for Best Actor for *Big*; stars in *The 'Burbs* and *Turner & Hooch*.

1990—Stars in *Joe Versus the Volcano* and *Bonfire of the Vanities*; son Chester is born.

1992—Narrates and makes a small appearance in *Radio Flyer*; has a supporting role in *A League of Their Own*; directs an episode of HBO's *Tales of the Crypt*.

1993—Stars in *Sleepless in Seattle* and *Philadelphia*; directs an episode of *Fallen Angels* and an episode of the television series *A League of Their Own*.

1994—Wins Oscar for Best Actor for *Philadelphia*; stars in *Forrest Gump*.

1995—Wins second Oscar for Best Actor for *Forrest Gump*; stars in *Apollo 13*; is the voice of Sheriff Woody in the computer-animated film *Toy Story*; son Truman Theodore is born.

1996—Writes and directs *That Thing You Do*.

1998—Is executive producer of *From the Earth to the Moon*, a twelve-part HBO miniseries; stars in *Saving Private Ryan* and *You've Got Mail*.

1999—Nominated for an Oscar for Best Actor for *Saving Private Ryan*; wins an Emmy award for Outstanding Miniseries for *From the Earth to the Moon*; is honored by the American Museum of the Moving Image; is the voice of Sheriff Woody for *Toy Story 2*; stars in *The Green Mile*.

2000—Stars in *Cast Away*.

## A Selected List

*He Knows You're Alone*, 1980
*Splash*, 1984
*Bachelor Party*, 1984
*The Man with One Red Shoe*, 1985
*Volunteers*, 1985
*The Money Pit*, 1986
*Nothing in Common*, 1986
*Every Time We Say Goodbye*, 1986
*Dragnet*, 1987
*Big*, 1988
*Punchline*, 1988
*The 'Burbs*, 1989
*Turner & Hooch*, 1989
*Joe Versus the Volcano*, 1990
*Bonfire of the Vanities*, 1990
*Radio Flyer*, 1992
*A League of Their Own*, 1992
*Sleepless in Seattle*, 1993
*Philadelphia*, 1993
*Forrest Gump*, 1994
*Apollo 13*, 1995
*Toy Story*, 1995
*That Thing You Do*, 1996 (also writer and director)
*Saving Private Ryan*, 1998
*You've Got Mail*, 1998
*Toy Story 2*, 1999
*The Green Mile*, 1999
*Cast Away*, 2000

## Chapter 1. "Stupid Is as Stupid Does"

All the quotations in this chapter are taken from the movie *Forrest Gump*, Paramount Pictures, 1994.

## Chapter 2. The New Kid in School

1. Kevin Sessums, "Tom Terrific," *Vanity Fair*, June 1994, p. 150.

2. Jeanne Wolf, "New Direction for Tom," *New York Daily News*, September 29, 1996.

3. David Sheff, "Playboy Interview: Tom Hanks," *Playboy*, March 1989, pp. 59ff.

4. Diana Maychick, "Tom Hanks, the Reluctant Hunk," *Mademoiselle*, November 1986, p. 96.

5. Mary Murphy, "Tom Hanks: One Hunk Who Refuses to Go Hollywood," *Cosmopolitan*, March 1987, p. 226.

6. Fred Schruers, "Tom Hanks Is the Nicest Wise Guy in Hollywood," *New York Daily News*, July 21, 1985.

7. Mal Vincent, "Tom Hanks on 'That Thing You Do,'" Knight-Ridder/Tribune News Service, October 9, 1996, p. 1009K5194.

8. Kathy Passero, "That Thing He Does: The Perpetual Appeal of Tom Hanks," *Biography Magazine*, July 1998, p. 34.

9. David DeNicolo, "Right Behind Mr. Nice Guy Lurks an Edgy Tom Hanks," *The New York Times*, June 20, 1993, p. H27.

10. Hilary de Vries, "Mr. Cute Guy Grows Up," *Boston Globe*, January 2, 1994.

11. Karen S. Schneider, "Tom on Top," *People*, August 3, 1998, p. 84.

12. Bill Zehme, "Mr. Big," *Rolling Stone*, June 30, 1988, p. 68.

13. Sessums, p. 151.

14. Candace Burke-Block, *"Big* Looks Like Another Big Hit for Tom Hanks, Happy Newlywed," *Buffalo News*, June 5, 1988.

15. Eric Sherman and Susan Granger, "The Clean-cut Kids," *Ladies' Home Journal*, April 1987, p. 183.

16. "Celebrity Profile," E! cable television network, September 5, 1999.

17. Linda Lee, *Tom Hanks* (New York: Time Inc., 1999), p. 29.

18. "Tom Hanks: Diving into Films with Splash!" *Teen Magazine*, March 1984, p. 53.

19. Judy Markey, "Honing in on Hanks," *Cosmopolitan*, July 1985, p. 100.

20. David Blum, "Tom Hanks's Real Splash," *New York*, July 28, 1986, p. 39.

21. Sid Smith, "Shucks, Tom Hanks Is Just a Likable Guy Who's Made a Splash in Movies," *Chicago Tribune*, July 27, 1986.

22. Henry Sheehan, "Leader of the Pack," *Orange County Register* (Santa Ana, Calif.), October 4, 1996.

## Chapter 3. An Ordinary Guy

1. Roy Trakin, *Tom Hanks: Journey to Stardom* (New York: St. Martin's Press, 1995), p. 35.

2. Beverly Walker, "Hanks to You," *Film Comment*, March–April 1989, p. 18.

3. David Sheff, "Playboy Interview: Tom Hanks," *Playboy*, March 1989, pp. 59ff.

4. Steven Rea, "His Splash in Comedies Isn't Over," *Philadelphia Inquirer*, August 21, 1985.

5. Rick Lyman, "Hanks Takes the Plunge and Has a Hit," *Philadelphia Inquirer*, March 15, 1984.

6. Sean Mitchell, "Will 'Party' Be Tom Hanks' Next Splash?" *Los Angeles Herald Examiner*, June 27, 1984.

7. Henry Sheehan, "Leader of the Pack," *Orange County Register* (Santa Ana, Calif.), October 4, 1996.

8. Karen S. Schneider, "Tom on Top," *People*, August 3, 1998, p. 84.

9. "How to Look Like a Page Out of Esquire," *Esquire*, March 1987, p. F50.

10. Steve K. Walz, "Prime-time Bombs," *TV Guide*, June 30, 1990, p. 11.

11. Robert MacKenzie, "Review," *TV Guide*, January 10, 1981, p. 30.

12. Trakin, p. 49.

13. Richard Corliss, "The Bodies in Question," *Time*, November 3, 1980, p. 100.

14. Roger D. Friedman, "Tom Hanks," *New York Daily News*, June 20, 1993.

15. John J. O'Connor, "TV: 'Mazes and Monsters,' Fantasy," *The New York Times*, December 28, 1982, p. C12.

16. Todd McCarthy, "Auteur Opie," *Film Comment*, May–June, 1984, p. 42.

17. Robert Goldberg, "Hanks a Throwback to Days of Sweetness, Style," *Florida Times-Union*, August 2, 1986.

18. Lyman.

19. Roger Ebert, "Thanks Hanks," *Playboy*, December 1994, pp. 142ff.

20. "Tom Hanks: Diving into Films with Splash!" *Teen Magazine*, March 1984, p. 53.

## Chapter 4. A Filming Frenzy

1. Ralph Novak, "The Man with One Red Shoe," *People*, August 5, 1985, p. 8.

2. Bruce Weber and David Wild, "Big Again," *Vogue*, July 1993, p. 150.

3. David Ansen, "A Stand-up Guy," *Newsweek*, September 26, 1988, p. 57.

4. Ibid.

5. Weber and Wild, p. 150.

6. Ibid.

7. David Sheff, "Playboy Interview: Tom Hanks," *Playboy*, March 1989, pp. 59ff.

8. Mary Murphy, "Tom Hanks: One Hunk Who Refuses to Go Hollywood," *Cosmopolitan*, March 1987, p. 226.

9. Roger D. Friedman, "Tom Hanks," *New York Daily News*, June 20, 1993.

10. Beverly Walker, "Hanks to You," *Film Comment*, March–April 1989, p. 18.

11. Murphy, p. 227.

12. Sid Smith, "Lasting Laughs: Tom Hanks, Actor, Moves Beyond Light Comedy," *Chicago Tribune*, May 29, 1988.

13. James Verniere, "Hanks: The New Jimmy Stewart?" *Boston Herald*, May 29, 1988.

14. Robert Goldberg, "Hanks a Throwback to Days of Sweetness, Style," *Florida Times-Union*, August 2, 1986.

15. Lynn Darling, "He's Just a Cockeyed Optimist," *Newsday*, June 28, 1987.

16. Alan Carter, "'Big' Man," *New York Daily News*, May 28, 1988.

17. Ibid.

18. Darling.

19. "How to Look Like a Page Out of Esquire," *Esquire*, March 1987, p. F49.

20. Kristine McKenna, "Can Hanks' Likability Withstand a Gay Role?" *Chicago Tribune*, January 9, 1994, sec. 13, p. 25.

21. David Blum, "Tom Hanks's Real Splash," *New York*, July 28, 1986, p. 38.

22. Kevin Sessums, "Tom Terrific," *Vanity Fair*, June 1994, p. 150.

## Chapter 5. The *Big* Year

1. Bill Zehme, "Mr. Big," *Rolling Stone*, June 30, 1988, p. 42.

2. Candace Burke-Block, "*Big* Looks Like Another Big Hit for Tom Hanks, Happy Newlywed," *Buffalo News*, June 5, 1988.

3. James Verniere, "Hanks: The New Jimmy Stewart?" *Boston Herald*, May 29, 1988.

4. Jack Garner, "Tom Hanks Is Making It Big," *Democrat and Chronicle* (Rochester, N.Y.), May 29, 1988.

5. Gerald Clarke, "The Eternal Cutup at Work," *Time*, June 6, 1988, p. 79.

6. Peter Travers, "Big," *People*, June 6, 1988, pp. 16ff.

7. Paul Freeman, "To Spice Up Familiar Plot: Add Tom Hanks," *San Francisco Examiner*, May 29, 1988.

8. Garner.

9. Peter Keough, "Tom Hanks in Big Time: The Hot Comic Star Creates His Own Little World," *Chicago Sun Times*, May 29, 1988.

10. Freeman.

11. Zehme, p. 68.

12. Ibid.

13. Ibid.

14. Hal Mattern, "Tom Hanks Loves Comedy But Avoids Stand-up," *Arizona Republic*, October 5, 1988.

15. Ibid.

16. David Sheff, "Playboy Interview: Tom Hanks," *Playboy*, March 1989, pp. 59ff.

17. Mal Vincent, "Tom Hanks on 'That Thing You Do,'" Knight-Ridder/Tribune News Service, October 9, 1996, p. 1009K5194.

18. Sheff.

19. Mary Murphy, "Tom Hanks: One Hunk Who Refuses to Go Hollywood," *Cosmopolitan*, March 1987, p. 226.

20. Kevin Sessums, "Tom Terrific," *Vanity Fair*, June 1994, p. 150.

## Chapter 6. Into the Bonfire

1. Benjamin Svetkey, "Tom Hanks," *Entertainment Weekly*, December 31, 1993, pp. 28ff.

2. Nancy Anderson, "Tom Hanks: A Rare Talk with Hollywood's Hottest New Star," *Good Housekeeping*, May 1989, p. 172.

3. Jack Garner, "Tom Hanks Is Making It Big," *Democrat and Chronicle* (Rochester, N.Y.), May 29, 1988.

4. Candace Burke-Block, "*Big* Looks Like Another Big Hit for Tom Hanks, Happy Newlywed," *Buffalo News*, June 5, 1988.

5. Lynn Darling, "He's Just a Cockeyed Optimist," *Newsday*, June 28, 1987.

6. Beverly Walker, "Hanks to You," *Film Comment*, March–April 1989, p. 19.

7. David Kronke, "Hanks Is Hot, Hot, Hot About His Recent Films," *Dallas Times Herald*, March 4, 1990.

8. Stephen Schaefer, "Chances Are, Hanks Will Hit It 'Big' Again," *Boston Herald*, March 9, 1990.

9. Kronke.

10. Caryn James, "A Droll Buddy Who Drools and Eats a Stereo Speaker," *The New York Times*, July 28, 1989, p. C8.

11. Joe Logan, "The Very Hot Tom Hanks," *Philadelphia Inquirer*, March 11, 1990.

12. Lisa Schwarzbaum, Bronwen Hruska, and Ty Burr, "The Nice Man Cometh: Tom Hanks," *Entertainment Weekly*, July 9, 1993, pp. 14ff.

13. Ibid.

14. Geraldine Fabrikant, "Disappointed Warner Has No Year-End Hit, *The New York Times*, December 25, 1990, p. Λ43.

15. Mal Vincent, "Make-out Movie," *Virginian-Pilot* (Norfolk, Va.), June 24, 1993.

16. Bruce Weber and David Wild, "Big Again," *Vogue*, July 1993, p. 150.

17. Bart Mills, "Comic Actor Tom Hanks Takes on Roles with Real Emotion in *Sleepless in Seattle* and *Philadelphia*," *Boston Herald*, June 20, 1993.

18. Karen S. Schneider, "Tom on Top," *People*, August 3, 1998, p. 87.

19. Joe Rhodes, "Back From the Bonfire," *Los Angeles Times*, July 5, 1992.

20. Brian D. Johnson, "Peaking Tom," *Maclean's*, July 11, 1994, p. 53.

21. Schwarzbaum.

22. Kevin Sessums, "Tom Terrific," *Vanity Fair*, June 1994, p. 152.

## Chapter 7. Taking a Risk

1. Hilary de Vries, "Rita Wilson Best Supporting Wife?" *McCall's*, November 1995, pp. 118–119.

2. Benjamin Svetkey, "Mail Bonding," *Entertainment Weekly*, December 18, 1998, p. 28.

3. Kristine McKenna, "Can Hanks' Likability Withstand a Gay Role?" *Chicago Tribune*, January 9, 1994, sec. 13, p. 26.

4. Ibid.

5. Hilary de Vries, "Mr. Cute Guy Grows Up," *Boston Globe*, January 2, 1994.

6. David Quinlan, *Tom Hanks: A Career in Orbit* (London: B. T. Batsford, 1997), p. 72.

7. Mal Vincent, "Tom Hanks," *Virginian-Pilot* (Norfolk, Va.), January 13, 1994.

8. David DeNicolo, "Right Behind Mr. Nice Guy Lurks an Edgy Tom Hanks," *The New York Times*, June 20, 1993, p. H27.

9. Brian D. Johnson, "Peaking Tom," *Maclean's*, July 11, 1994, p. 54.

10. Roger Ebert, "Question of Justice," *Chicago Sun Times*, January 9, 1994.

11. Quinlan, p. 77.

12. "Tom Hanks," *Mr. Showbiz*, n.d. <http://mrshowbiz.go.com/people/tomhanks/content/Bio.html> (February 15, 2000).

13. Barry Caine, "Acting on Faith," *Daily Review* (Hayward, Calif.), July 8, 1994.

14. Barry Koltnow, "Tom Hanks," *Orange County Register* (Santa Ana, Calif.), July 3, 1994.

15. Ibid.

## Chapter 8. Journey into Space

1. Kevin Sessums, "Tom Terrific," *Vanity Fair*, June 1994, p. 152.

2. Philip Wuntch, "Mr. Wonderful," *Dallas Morning News*, July 8, 1994.

3. Kathy Passero, "The Things He Does: The Perpetual Appeal of Tom Hanks," *Biography Magazine*, July 1998, p. 37.

4. Mal Vincent, "Show Some Gumption," *Virginian-Pilot* (Norfolk, Va.), July 6, 1994.

5. Brian D. Johnson, "Peaking Tom," *Maclean's*, July 11, 1994, p. 54.

6. Jeff Gordinier, "Tom Hanks," *Entertainment Weekly*, December 30, 1994, pp. 16ff.

7. "Tom Hanks & Rita Wilson," *People*, February 12, 1996, p. 167.

8. Karen S. Schneider, "Tom on Top," *People*, August 3, 1998, p. 89.

9. Mark Morrison, "Married to Mr. Nice Guy," *Ladies' Home Journal*, February 1995, p. 63.

10. Rene Rodriguez, "Tom Hanks Is Having a Blast," *Miami Herald*, June 25, 1995.

11. Pam Lambert, "Aces in Space," *People*, July 3, 1995, p. 73.

12. Skip Hollandsworth, "Shooting the Moon: The Inside Story of the Making of *Apollo 13* (New Feature Film Directed by Ron Howard)," *Texas Monthly*, July 1995, pp. 92ff.

13. "Hollywood Hotshots," *Biography*, A&E cable television network, August 5, 1998.

14. *Celebrity Profile*, E! cable television network, September 5, 1999.

15. Richard Corliss, "Hell of a Ride," *Time*, July 3, 1995, p. 53.

16. Ibid.

17. Lambert, p. 73.

18. Corliss, p. 51.

19. Lee Pfeiffer and Michael Lewis, *The Films of Tom Hanks* (Secaucus, N.J.: Carol Publishing Group, 1996), p. 192.

20. David Quinlan, *Tom Hanks: A Career in Orbit* (London: B. T. Batsford, 1997), p. 80.

21. Richard Corliss, "They're Alive!" *Time*, November 27, 1995, p. 96.

## Chapter 9. From Star to Superstar

1. Jeff Gordinier, "Hanks for the Memories," *Entertainment Weekly*, October 11, 1996, pp. 24ff.

2. Barry Koltnow, "Tom Hanks," *Orange County Register* (Santa Ana, Calif.), July 3, 1994.

3. Mal Vincent, "Tom Hanks on 'That Thing You Do,'" Knight-Ridder/Tribune News Service, October 9, 1996, p. 1009K5194.

4. Jeanne Wolf, "New Directions for Tom," *New York Daily News*, September 29, 1996.

5. Vincent, p. 1009K5194.

6. Jane Wollman Rusoff, "The Mr. Showbiz Interview," *Mr. Showbiz*, n.d., <http://www.mrshowbiz.com/interviews/274_1.html> (February 15, 2000).

7. Joe Leydon, "That Tom Hanks Thing," *Boston Globe*, September 29, 1996.

8. Gordinier.

9. Ibid.

10. Leah Rozen, "That Thing You Do!" (review), *People*, October 7, 1996, p. 19.

11. *Saving Private Ryan: The Men. The Mission. The Movie.* (New York: Newmarket Press, 1998), unnumbered pages.

12. *Time & Again*, MSNBC cable television network, May 31, 1999.

13. "Saving Private Ryan" (review), *People*, August 3, 1998, p. 25.

14. "Tom Hanks Lends Support to National World War II Memorial," n.d., <http://wwiimemorial.com/hankspsas.htm> (February 15, 2000).

## Chapter 10. Honoring Hanks

1. Jim Caruso, "Tom of Their Lives: In New York, Friends Applaud Hanks's Homegrown Gumption," *In Style*, August 1, 1999, p. 124.

2. Karen S. Schneider, "Tom on Top," *People*, August 3, 1998, p. 89.

3. Richard Corliss and Cathy Booth, "Tom Terrific," *Time*, December 21, 1998, p. 77.

4. Walter Scott, "Personality Parade," *Parade Magazine*, June 27, 1999, p. 2.

## Further Reading

Corliss, Richard, and Cathy Booth. "Tom Terrific." *Time*, December 21, 1998, pp. 70–77.

Lanzen Harris, Laurie, ed. *Biography Today 1996 Annual Cumulation*. Detroit: Omnigraphics, Inc., 1996, pp. 145–155.

Lee, Linda. *Tom Hanks*. New York: Time, Inc., 1999.

Passero, Kathy. "That Thing He Does: The Perpetual Appeal of Tom Hanks." *Biography Magazine*, July 1998, pp. 30–37.

Pfeiffer, Lee, and Michael Lewis. *The Films of Tom Hanks*. Secaucus, N.J.: Carol Publishing Group, 1996.

Quinlan, David. *Tom Hanks: A Career in Orbit*. London: B. T. Batsford Ltd., 1998.

Trakin, Roy. *Tom Hanks: Journey to Stardom*. New York: St. Martin's Press, 1995.

### On the Internet

<http://mrshowbiz.go.com/people/tomhanks/content/Bio.html>

<http://www.moviething.com/bios/tomhanks>

<http://www.fansites.com/tom_hanks.html>

Page numbers for photographs are in **boldface** type.